Graphic Design
BASICS

Working With
Words &
Pictures

Lori Siebert **&** *Mary Cropper*

**NORTH
LIGHT
BOOKS**

Cincinnati, Ohio

This book is dedicated to those
we love and who love us—
Steve and Kenzie Siebert
and Evelyn Cropper
and Miss Trygve.

Our thanks to:
Diana Martin, Greg Albert
and everyone else at North Light
who made this book happen.
And especially to all the talented designers
who so generously supplied their work
for making it beautiful.

Printed and bound in Mexico.

This hardcover edition of *Working With Words & Pictures* features a "self-jacket" that eliminates the need for a separate dust jacket. It provides sturdy protection for your book while it saves paper, trees and energy.

97 96 95 94 93   5 4 3 2 1

Library of Congress Cataloging-in-Publication Data
Siebert, Lori
    Working with words and pictures / Lori Siebert & Mary Cropper. — 1st ed.
        p. cm. — (Graphic design basics)
    Includes index.
    ISBN 0-89134-437-3
        1. Printing, Practical—Layout.   I. Cropper, Mary.   II. Title.   III. Series.
Z246.S562   1993
686.2'252—dc20   93-24619
                                                          CIP

Edited by Greg Albert
Designed by Lori Siebert, Lisa Ballard and Paul Neff

The permissions on the following page constitute an extension of this copyright page.

Permissions

The following artwork is used by permission of the copyright holder.

Adam, Filippo & Associates: p. 59 © National Steel Corporation. Photographer: Harry Giglio.

Alexander Isley Design: pp. 13, 66, 89 © Alexander Isley Design. Art director and designer: Alexander Isley. P. 89 only: designer: Alexander Knowlton; photographer: Jim Bush.

Ambassador Foundation—Creative Services: p. 6 © 1991 Ambassador Foundation. Designer: Rex Pieper.

Arndt Photography/Fallon McElligott: p. 24 © Icebox Framing. Photographer: Jim Arndt.

Atlanta Art and Design: p. 73 © Atlanta Art and Design. Art director and designer: Mark Koudys; illustrator: Louis Fishauf.

Bagby Design Incorporated: p. 51 © Bagby Design Incorporated. Designer: Steven Bagby; photographer: Charlie Westerman.

Barry Huey, Bullock and Cook Advertising: p. 104 © Barry Huey, Bullock and Cook. Photography © 1991 Randy Mayor. Art director: Melanie Townsend-Colvin; photographer: Randy Mayor; creative director: Gracey Tillman; assoc. creative director: Bryan Chace.

Barsuhn Design Incorporated: p. 13 © Barsuhn Design Incorporated. Art director: Scott Barsuhn; designer: Sandra Harper.

Bennett Peji Design: p. 103 © 1991 Bennett Peji. Designer: Bennett Peji.

BlackDog: p. 78 © 1988 Mark Fox/BlackDog. Art director: Paul Huber/Altman & Manley; designer and illustrator: Mark Fox.

Borders, Perrin & Norrander: p. 69 © Borders, Perrin & Norrander. Art director: Tim Parker; photographer: Mark Hooper; creative director: Bill Borders.

Bostonia Magazine: p. 73 © Trustees of Boston University. Art director and designer: Douglas Parker; illustrator: Mark Fisher.

BYU Graphics: p. 118 © Brigham Young University. Art director, designer and illustrator: McRay Magleby; illustrator: David Eliason.

Catt Lyon Design: p. 50 © 1990 Xavier University. Designers: Charleen Catt Lyon and Suzanne Parkey.

Clifford Selbert Design: p. 120 © 1991 Clifford Selbert Design. Designer: Melanie Lowe; photographer: Francine Zaslow.

Clifford Stoltze Design: p. 25 © Clifford Stoltze Design. Designer: Clifford Stoltze.

Concrete: p. 10 © Concrete. Designers: Jilly Simons, David Robson and Cindy Chang; photographer: Kevin Anderson.

Cordella Design, Inc.: pp. 34-35 © T-Cell Sciences and George Petrakes. Art director and designer: Andree Cordella; photographer: George Petrakes.

Crosby Associates: p. 8 © 1990 Crosby Associates and Patti Green Illustration. Art director: Bart Crosby; designer: Carl Wohlt; illustrator: Patti Green.

DDB Needham Worldwide: p. 84 © Bermuda Department of Tourism. Art director: Dennis Steven; executive creative directors: Bob Mackall and Jack Mariucci.

Design II: p. 12 © KCPA. Designer: Robb Springfield.

DiDonato Associates: p. 121 © 1992 DiDonato Associates Inc. Art director and designer: Peter DiDonato; designers: Donald Childs and Kelli Evans; photographer: Herman Leonard.

Drenntel Doyle Partners: pp. 22, 66, 79 © Drenntel Doyle Partners.

Dugald Stermer: p. 36 © 1988 Mountain Lion Coalition & Dugald Stermer. Art director, designer and illustrator: Dugald Stermer.

Earl Gee Design: p. 102 © 1992 Earl Gee Design. Art director, designer and illustrator: Earl Gee; designer: Fani Chung.

Earle Palmer Brown/Atlanta: p. 75 © Earle Palmer Brown/Atlanta.

Elizabeth J. Merrin: p.-16 © Merrin Information Services, Inc.

Ellen East: p. 18 © Cox Enterprises, Inc.

Fallon McElligott: p. 85 © 1990 Fallon McElligott. Art director: Tom Lichtenheld; photographer: Mark LaFavor.

Frankfurt Gips Balkind: pp. 7, 13, 21, 92 © Frankfurt Gips Balkind. P. 7 only: © 1991 MCI Communications Corporation. Art director: Kent Hunter; designer: Riki Sethiadi; illustrators: Brian Cronin, John Hersey and Philip Anderson; photographers: Geof Spear, Scott Morgan, Heungman, Pete McArthur and David McGlynn. P. 13 only: art directors: Aubrey Balkind and Kent Hunter; designer: Thomas Bricker. P. 21 only: art director: Kent Hunter; designer: Kin Yuen; photographers: Boyd Webb, Mark Klett, Adam Fuss, Robert Frank, Harry Callahan, Joseph Koudelka and Timothy Greenfield-Sanders (portraits). P. 92 only: © 1991 Seagram's Ltd. Art directors: Kent Hunter and Aubrey Balkind; designer: Benjamin Bailey; illustrators: Thessy Mehrain and Josh Goshfield; photographers: Julie Powell, Hans Neleman, Hugh Kreschmer, Henrik Kam, Cheryl Kordlik and Dan Borris.

Frazer Design: pp. 23, 82 © Craig Frazer. Designer: Craig Frazer. P. 23 only: photography © John Casado.

Gable Design Group: p. 103 © Gable Design Group. Art director and designer: Tony Gable; designer: Jana Nishi; illustrator: Karin Yamagiwa.

Geer Design, Inc.: pp. 9, 41, 87 © Geer Design, Inc. Art director and designer: Mark Geer. P. 9 only: designer and illustrator: Morgan Bomar; photographer: Chris Shinn. P. 41 only: illustrator: Lane Smith; photographer: Mike Hallaway. P. 87 only: photographer: Terry Asker.

Gil Shuler Graphic Design: p. 120 © Gil Shuler Graphic Design. Art director, designer and illustrator: Gil Shuler.

Goodby, Berlin & Silverstein: pp. 40, 71, 80. Creative directors: Jeffrey Goodby and Rich Silverstein. P. 40 only: © 1990 Clarks of England Inc. Art director: Tracy Wong; illustrator: Greg Dearth. P. 71 only: © 1990 The Nature Company. Art director: Tracy Wong; photographers: Gerry Bybee and Barry Robinson. P. 80 only: © 1989 San Francisco Newspaper Agency. Art director: Steve Stone; photographer: Dan Escobar.

Graffito: pp. 108, 114 © 1992 Graffito, Inc. P. 140 only: photographer: Ed Whitman/Lightstruck Studios. P. 114 only: art director: Tim Thompson; designer and illustrator: Joe Parisi.

Graphica, Inc.: pp. 19, 93 © Graphica, Inc. P. 19 only: art director and designer: Cindy Schnell.

Henderson Advertising, Inc./Atlanta: p. 74 © Henderson Advertising, Inc./Atlanta. Art director: Bart Cleveland.

Hornall Anderson Design Works: pp. 38, 47, 49, 116 © Hornall Anderson Design Works. Pp. 38 and 49 only: designers: Jack Anderson and Mary Hermes. P. 49 only: designers: Jack Anderson, Denise Weir and Lian Ng. P. 116 only: designers: Jack Anderson, Julia LaPine and Lian Ng.

Howard, Merrell & Partners, Inc.: p. 85 © 1992 CIBA-GEIGY Corporation. Art director: Susan Jones; photographer: Buck Holzemer; creative director: Gary Knutson.

Imprint Graphic Design Associates: p. 34 © Institute of Ecosystems Studies, New York. Art director and designer: Sara Seagull; designer: Susan Mason; illustrator: Amy Melson; photographers: Manuel Rodriguez and Ed Roy; creative director: Bill Beirne;

charts and map production: Jared Schneidman Design.

Ingalls, Quinn & Johnson: p. 69 © 1991 Converse Inc. and Hiro Studio. Art director: Marc Gallucci; photography: Hiro Studio.

James A. Hoff Design: p. 119 © James A. Hoff Design. Designer: James A. Hoff.

Kienberger Design: p. 16 © Carpenters/Contractors Cooperation Committee. Art director and designer: Tom Kienberger.

Kym Abrams Design: p. 10 © Kym Abrams Design. Art director: Kym Abrams; designer: Barry Deck; illustrator: Quong Ho.

Larry Vigon Studio: p. 102 © Larry Vigon Studio.

Lawler Ballard Van Durand: p. 104 © 1992 Lawler Ballard Van Durand. Art director: Don Harbor; photographer: Billy Brown.

Liska and Associates, Inc.: p. 72 © Liska and Associates, Inc.

Louise Fili Ltd.: p. 17 © Louise Fili Ltd. Designer: Louise Fili; illustrator: Mark Summers.

Mann Bukvic Associates: pp. 7, 37, 68 © Mann Bukvic Associates. Creative director: David Bukvic; art director and designer: Cathy Bertke. P. 43a only: art director and designer: Diane Durban.

Margo Chase Design: p. 56 © 1990 Margo Chase Design. Art director and designer: Margo Chase; designer: Nancy Ogami.

Mark Oldach Design: pp. 27, 110, 111 © Mark Oldach Design. Art director and designer: Mark Oldach. P. 27 only: designer: Mark Meyer.

Meldrum & Fewsmith: p. 80 © Meldrum & Fewsmith. Art director and designer: Bill Schwartz; illustrator: Dave Fitch; creative director: Chris Perry.

Metropolitan Home Magazine: p. 56 © 1990 Meredith Corporation. All rights reserved. Art director and designer: Don Morris; designers: C. Kayo Der Sarkissian, Robin Terra, Susan Foster and Dorothy O'Connor; photographer: Lizzie Himmel.

Michael Brock Design: p. 39 © Michael Brock Design. Art director: Michael Brock; designer: Holly Caporale; photographer: Tim Street Porter.

Morla Design: pp. 83, 116, 118 © Morla Design, Inc. Designers: Jennifer Morla and Sharrie Brooks. P. 116 only: designer and illustrator: Jennifer Morla.

Mullen Advertising: p. 72 © 1992 Malden Mills Industries, Inc. Art director: Brenda Dziadzio; photographer: John Holt Studio.

Nike Design: p. 81 © Nike Design. Art director, designer and illustrator: John Norman; illustrator: Anton Kimball.

Northlich Stolley LaWarre: pp. 68, 105. P. 68 only: © 1992 The Jewish Hospitals of Cincinnati. Art director: Joe Stryker; illustrator: Toby Lay; photographer: Ron Rack. P. 105 only: © 1990 Northlich Stolley LaWarre. Art directors: Don Perkins and Diane Farris; photography: Teri Studios.

OMON: p. 84 © 1992 Toyota Motor Corporate Services of North America, Inc. Creative directors: Paul Bernasconi and Zodd Martin.

Paul Neff: p. 117 © 1992 Paul Neff. Designer: Paul Neff.

Pentagram: pp. 11, 16, 27, 50-51, 94 © Pentagram. Art director: Kit Hinrichs. P. 11 only: designer: Susan Tsuchiya; photographer: John Blaustein. P. 16 only: designer: Terri Driscoll; photographer: Steven A. Heller. P. 33 only: designer: Belle How; illustrator: F. Schuyler Mathews. Pp. 50-51 only: designer: Belle How; illustrator: Ed Lindlof; photographer: Steve Firebaugh.

Pentagram Design: pp. 33, 121 © Pentagram Design.

Designer: Paula Scher. P. 121 only: illustrator: Dugald Stermer.

Peterson & Company: p. 21 © Peterson & Company. Designer: Scott Paramski.

Primo Angeli, Inc.: p. 79 © Primo Angeli, Inc. Art director: Primo Angeli; designer: Mark Crumpacker.

RBMM: p. 4 © RBMM. Art director and designer: Brian Boyd; illustrator: Gary Templin.

Richard Poulin Design Group Inc.: p. 106 © Richard Poulin Design Group Inc. Art director and designer: Richard Poulin.

Rolling Stone Magazine: pp. 26, 77, 86 © Rolling Stone Magazine. Art director: Fred Woodward. P. 26 only: designer: Catherine Gilmore-Barnes; photographer: Herb Ritts. P. 77 top only: designer: Gail Anderson. P. 77 bottom only: designers: Gail Anderson and Fred Woodward; lettered by Anita Karl. P. 86 only: designer: Debra Bishop; photographer: Herb Ritts; lettered by Anita Karl.

Runyan Hinsche Associates: p. 15 © Runyan Hinsche Associates. Art director: Gary Hinsche.

Samata Associates: pp. 17, 19, 26, 34 © Samata Associates. Art directors: Pat and Greg Samata; photographer: Mark Joseph. P. 17 only: designer: Pat Samata. P. 19 only: designer: Jim Hardy; computer design: KC Yoon. P. 26 only: designers: Pat and Greg Samata. P. 34 only: designer: Pat Samata.

Schmeltz & Warren: p. 57 © Schmeltz & Warren. Art director and designer: Crit Warren; photographers: Larry Hamill, D.R. Goff, Ted Rice and George C. Anderson.

Scott Hull Associates: p. 44 © 1992 John Patrick/Scott Hull Associates. Illustrator: John Patrick.

Sibley/Peteet Design, Inc.: pp. 33, 78 © Sibley/Peteet Design, Inc. P. 33 only: art director and designer: Don Sibley. P. 84 only: art director and designer: Rex Peteet; creative director: Bill Stitzel.

Skolos/Wedell, Inc.: p. 113 © Skolos/Wedell, Inc. Designer: Nancy Skolos.

Stein Robaire Helen: p. 24 © Roland Corporation U.S. Art director: Steve Levit.

Supon Design Group, Inc.: pp. 103, 114 © Supon Design Group, Inc. Art director: Supon Phornirunlit. P. 103 only: designer: Dave Prescott. P. 114 only: designer: Rick Heffner.

THARP DID IT: p. 32 © THARP DID IT and Kelly O'Connor. Photographer: Kelly O'Connor.

The Pushpin Group: p. 67 © The Pushpin Group. Art director and designer: Seymour Chwast; designer: Roxanne Slimak.

The Riordon Design Group Inc.: pp. 38, 64 © 1990 The Riordon Design Group Inc.

Thirst: p. 5 © 1989 Thirst. Designers: Rick Valicenti and Michael Giammanco.

Thomas Ryan Design: p. 46 © Thomas Ryan Design. Art director: Thomas Ryan; designer: Cathy Wayland.

W. Joseph Gagnon Design Associates: p. 43 © W. Joseph Gagnon Design Associates. Designer: W. Joseph Gagnon.

Waters Design Associates, Inc.: pp. 14-15, 65, 70, 109 © Waters Design Associates, Inc. Art director: John Waters. P. 14-15 only: designers: Bob Kellerman and John Waters. P. 65 only: designer: Carol Bouyoucos. P. 70 only: designer: Dana Gonsalves. P. 109 only: designer: Carol Bouyoucos.

Whitehouse & Company: p. 14 © Whitehouse & Company. Art director: Roger Whitehouse.

Zender & Associates, Inc.: pp. 6, 107 © Zender & Associates, Inc. P. 6 only: art director and designer: Darla Haven. P. 107 only: art director and designer: Priscilla A. W. Fisher.

Contents

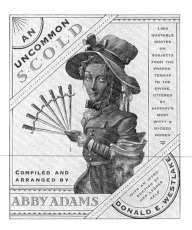

Chapter Three: Putting It All Together

Now that we've looked at the building blocks—type and visuals—let's look at ways to combine them most effectively. In this chapter, we'll show you how to shape layouts that present your message clearly and attractively.

Chapter Four: More Good Examples

This chapter presents different types of pieces done by a variety of designers to introduce numerous options for making good layouts. You'll get ideas for ways you can make what you've learned in this book work on any project.

Index

To Our Readers

Working with words and pictures—type and visuals (illustrations, photos and graphic elements)—in a layout is like working a jigsaw puzzle, but you get to choose the sizes, shapes and colors of the pieces. You even choose where the pieces go and how they fit together. That's why making a layout is so much fun.

What choices do you have? Plenty. Because words communicate through both their content and their appearance, what the type looks like may be as important as what it says. In the first chapter of this book, you'll learn many ways to make type an attractive, effective communication tool. The typeface, size, style and even the amount of leading you use can send a message to your readers.

Because visuals communicate messages quickly and memorably, they must be chosen with great care, especially since there are so many different types of visuals you can use. In the second chapter, you'll discover how to use illustrations, photos, clip art, charts and graphs, and graphic elements such as rules and borders to not only beautify but also to help get your message across.

How do you decide what to use and where it should go? How do you know if you've put your layout together right? You must consider the format, audience, environment and intent of the project. Then you need to bring order to the type and visuals needed to communicate your message. In the third chapter, you'll find dozens of ideas for taking your layouts from the initial, carefully thought out concepts through the process of shaping and refining until you have the right layout. You'll discover how to choose the best format for a piece and how to use a grid to bring order without limiting your layout options.

Once you've mastered the basics, you'll want to explore numerous options for making layouts. In chapter four, you'll find different types of pieces done by a variety of designers that introduce numerous options for making layouts. This wide range of approaches can serve as a springboard for expanding the boundaries of your own design and layouts. Once you've explored these new ideas, take in everything else around you—signs, posters, fabrics, anything that sparks a great idea for a layout. Most important of all, experiment constantly. Don't be afraid to try something new; that's the best way to grow.

Chapter 1
Words

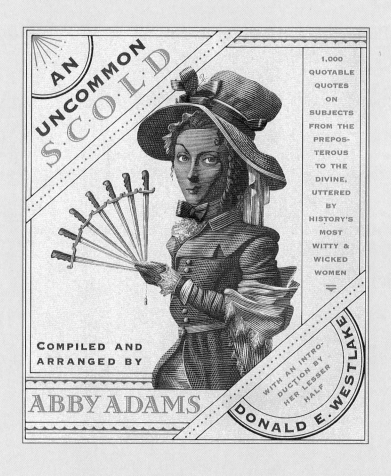

The words in a layout—headlines, body copy, captions, logotypes, etc.—play a key role in communicating your message to its audience. That means the audience must be able to read and understand the typeset words. But type can be—in fact, it must be—attractive to effectively put across its message.

Words communicate through their content and their appearance. The size and treatment of the copy and headlines show readers what is most important and what should be read first. The typeface and type style can tell your readers what the tone or mood of a piece is before they read a word.

Design all type in your layouts for maximum impact. Plan every aspect—leading, placement, type treatment—with great care. Then your audience will feel compelled to read your message.

Type can even be an important graphic element. Captions and pull quotes, especially, are often set in a different face or given a unique alignment so they will contrast with the other type on the page. This adds interest and helps pull the reader into the piece.

This chapter shows how to make type an attractive, effective communication tool.

Headlines

A headline must stop readers and persuade them to read your piece. Headlines can be visually interesting, verbally interesting or, best of all, both when what the headline says is reinforced by how it's treated visually. When a headline is verbally interesting ("Man Bites Dog") or strictly factual ("10th Annual Golf Outing Friday"), you can set it in large, strong type and let the words do the work.

Sometimes a headline will need a special treatment to make it more attractive ("Dog Bites Man") or to help the reader interpret it ("Let It Be"). Other times the words in a headline are expressive and it is easy to emphasize special words, with one or more set in a different size, style or typeface ("top," "big" and "intensive" are good candidates).

Headlines communicate the personality of a printed piece. If you're doing a newsletter for a day-care center, your headlines should look fun, playful or whimsical. You can achieve these or other looks through your choice of typeface and the arrangement of headlines and their graphic treatment. For the day-care newsletter you could set a headline in a friendly typeface such as *New Century Schoolbook* or print it in a bright color.

Profile: Dan Boatwright

At six feet, four inches and 240 pounds, teacher Dan Thomas Boatwright looks as though he must have played left tackle for Texas A&M, his alma mater. Instead, his interests took him into more unusual and less aggressive hobbies, such as trout fishing—he ties his own flies—and falconry.

"I get outdoors every chance I get," says Boatwright, with great enthusiasm. This includes summer trips to Idaho or Yellowstone to hunt and fish with Tom Lutken, Episcopal School's Wilderness Director, as well as weekend walks in the countryside in Duncanville where Boatwright lives. His love of the out-of-doors, and his knowledge about it—gained through academic training and personal experience—contribute greatly to his teaching of upper school Biology and Earth Science classes.

A Dallas native, Dan Boatwright attended Sunset High School, earned his undergraduate degree in Zoology and Microbiology at Texas A&M, and completed an M.S. in Molecular Biology from the University of Texas at Dallas. During the summer between high school and college he was selected to attend the Texas Maritime Academy. Sponsored by A&M, the academy takes students on a 10-week cruise, to distant ports including Oslo, Amsterdam, Gibraltar, and San Juan, Puerto Rico. Boatwright completed two college-level courses in between work in the engine room or on deck and tours of the ports-of-call. "I found out I didn't like sailing very much," he recalls, mentioning a serious case of seasickness provoked by the ship's passage near a hurricane.

While in high school Boatwright seriously pursued his outdoors interests. He earned the rank of Eagle Scout, and he took up falconry as a hobby. "The idea is to train a bird to come back to you when you call it," he explains. "It's a form of hunting; instead of using a dog, you use a bird of prey."

When Boatwright finished graduate school he worked first as a research technician in

Dan Boatwright and his feathered friend

The format of this private school's newsletter is a take-off on a notebook. The handwritten headline heightens the feel and flavor of the piece, reminding readers of penmanship practice sheets, schoolroom essays—and the values of traditional, quality education.

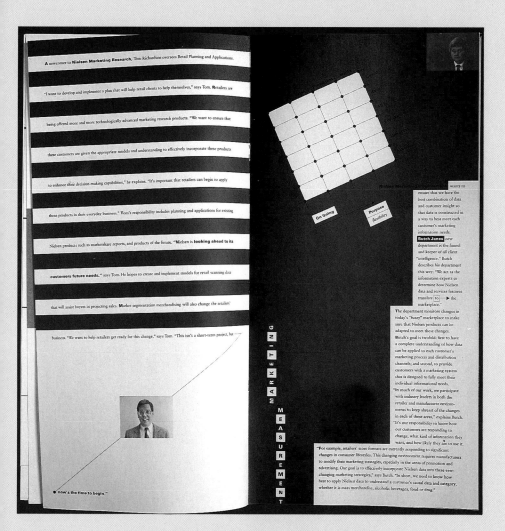

Unlike the piece on the facing page, this brochure has a high tech, high contrast, geometric look. That's why placing the heads inside checkerboards works well here. It also adds a somewhat playful note to a piece that otherwise might look too stiff or hard.

When designing headlines:

• Choose a headline typeface that reflects the personality you want the piece to project. (A delicate script face such as *Zapf Chancery* wouldn't work well in an ad for rugged work clothes.)

• Make sure they contrast sufficiently with the surrounding copy. (If all the type is the same face, size and color, how can readers see what the levels of information are?)

• Try placing a headline inside a shape, but only when that shape reinforces the piece's message.

• Set them larger than body copy so they do stand out, but don't make them so large that they overwhelm the copy.

• Always break long headlines so they can be read easily ("Fireman Risks Life to/Save Cat Caught in Tree").

• Set them so they run the whole width of the article, if possible.

• Don't set long headlines in all caps, center them or hyphenate them. It makes them too hard to read.

• Make sure that the headline and any visuals convey the same message.

• Treat them consistently throughout a brochure or newsletter. (Don't change the typeface, style or size of headlines to "fix" an awkward spread, for example.)

Headlines

Even though these headlines are short and set fairly small relative to the type size of the copy, they are brought out visually by the heavy black bands beneath them. This graphic treatment ties the headlines to the masthead, which also has a band beneath it.

Fall 1987

On Line

quarterly newsletter

CTC

Contents

IPS Goes Off-shore

Constructing an operator workstation for off-shore, pipeline and remote station applications has been a challenge due to harsh environments and the constraints of 12- or 24-volt DC battery packs or other standby power sources. CTC's newest product, the IPS 2012/24 RoughNeck meets this challenge head-on.

The IPS 2012/24 RoughNeck offers all the benefits of the IPS 2000 operator interface modular system. It is a cost-effective, easy-to-use, standard solution to custom panels. The difference is the RoughNeck runs directly from 12- or 24-volt DC battery packs or other standby power sources.

For more information about the IPS 2012/24 RoughNeck, call your IPS sales representative or call Diana Tomlinson at 513-831-2340.

Quality is Top Priority

A Square D programming terminal sits across from an IBM PC. Test specifications are neatly piled on the desk next to y-connectors and a roll of coaxial cable. Crumpled M&M packages surround a copy of user documentation that looks like a Freshman English paper after being graded.

This is the domain of quality control. Where Mark Hensley writes 250 messages to test the ScreenWare2 Logic Editor, and Mary Ramsey uses an Electrostatic Discharge Gun and a Showering Arc Tester to test IPS 2000 modules. This is where documentation is read and reread, and lighted pushbuttons are pushed to their limits. This is where quality is defined and assured at CTC.

Two of CTC's principles "Commitment to Customers" and "Commitment to Excellence" make quality a top priority. The path to achieving quality starts with Marketing where the product function, environment, packaging and aesthetic requirements are defined. Engineering then takes over and designs a product that is reliable and easy-to-use.

From Engineering, the product and product documentation is handed over to Quality Control. It is at this point that quality systems engineers like Mary Ramsey and Mark Hensley design test plans and test specifications that will verify the product meets quality requirements and is bug-free.

Continued on page 2.

Domingo In U.S. Orchestra Conducting Debut

When Plácido Domingo performs on any stage in any capacity, he generates a special kind of excitement that begins to build as soon as the appearance is announced. His upcoming concerts, not as Tenor Plácido Domingo but as Maestro Plácido Domingo, conductor of the **Los Angeles Chamber Orchestra** at Ambassador on January 30 and February 2, are no exception. Ever since Ambassador's and LACO's brochures reached their respective patrons, we and the Chamber Orchestra have been receiving inquiries from fascinated concertgoers wanting details of this landmark occasion – his United States debut as conductor in a purely orchestral setting. In answer to those queries, LACO has announced a tentative program: a Rossini overture; Haydn's Sinfonia Concertante in B-Flat, Op. 84, featuring LACO principals Ralph Morrison, violin, Douglas Davis, cello, Allan Vogel, oboe, and Kenneth Munday,

bassoon; the Tchaikovsky Serenade for Strings; and possibly a Mozart symphony. We ask you not to hold Mr. Domingo too closely to this program, with *Virtuosi's* early copy deadline (September), some of these works may change.

Plácido Domingo's distinguished career as one of the world's most renowned tenors needs no review here. Suffice it to say that he can be heard in Southern California in January and February in the Los Angeles Music Center Opera's new production of *Carmen* and in a gala concert presented by Orange County's Opera Pacific on January 12. Other important appearances in 1991-92 have already included the opening of LAMCO's season in September in a special performance of *Madama Butterfly*; the Metropolitan Opera's season opener celebrating 25 years of the Met at Lincoln Center; and a new Met production of *La Fanciulla del West*, to be televised at a later date.

Naumburg Winners Announced

Ticket holders to Gold Medal concerts have been waiting for news of the outcome of the 1991 Naumburg Chamber Music and Viola competitions, the winners of which are scheduled to appear on February 10 and April 13, respectively. Regrettably, the 1991 Chamber Music winner is not able to participate in the series this season due to scheduling conflicts but will appear in a future year. As a replacement for that ensemble, the Walter W. Naumburg Foundation has offered us the 1989 winner, the outstanding **Peabody Trio**: violinist Violaine Melançon; cellist Bonnie Thron; and pianist Seth Knopp.

Formed in 1986 in San Francisco, the threesome began a full-time residency at the Peabody Institute in Baltimore in 1987 and took its name from that prestigious conservatory. The Trio's victory in the 1988 Baltimore Chamber Music Awards Competition, residencies at Tanglewood and Ravinia and concerts throughout the U.S. and Canada, including a 1990 New York debut at Alice Tully Hall, attest to the growing reputation of the

ensemble is enjoying. Equally promising is the recently announced winner of the 1991 Viola Competition, **Misha Amory**, who is currently a candidate for the Master of Music degree at the Juilliard School. Previous studies were at the Eastman School of Music, Yale University and in Berlin on a Fulbright Grant. He has already been soloist with the Boston Symphony and, as a participant in the Marlboro Festival since 1989, is scheduled to tour in the near future with Music from Marlboro.

Photos top to bottom:
The Peabody Trio,
Misha Amory.

CLAUDIO ARRAU
February 6, 1903
June 9, 1991

Called "the aristocrat of the keyboard," the Chilean-born pianist gave unsparingly of himself in programs of demanding virtuosity even into his octogenarian years. A renowned scholar and teacher and an erudite man of great musical and personal integrity, he will be best remembered for his powerful and insightful performances of Beethoven and Liszt and for the clarity and poetry of his Chopin, Schumann and Debussy.

Claudio Arrau appeared in recital at Ambassador on three occasions, most recently on February 18, 1986.

Pasadena Jazz Weekend Scores A Success

Lexus Sponsors Weekend and Sounds of Genius

Ambassador Foundation is pleased to announce the successful completion of its first Pasadena Jazz Weekend last August 24 and 25. The weekend, which featured performances by jazz greats Dizzy Gillespie, the Claude Bolling Big Band, Poncho Sanchez and the Harper Brothers, was made possible in large part by Lexus, the luxury division of Toyota Motor Sales, USA, title sponsor of the event. Radio stations KPCC and KLON cooperated in the presentation, net proceeds of which benefited the American Cancer Society.

In announcing the corporation's backing, Group Vice President and General Manager of Lexus, J. Davis Illingworth stated, "Lexus is proud to present the Pasadena Jazz Weekend. This sponsorship is an example of our ongoing commitment to enhancing the cultural lives of those who live and work in the communities in which we do business." An active supporter of the arts, Lexus has sponsored a host of events and organizations around the country, including the Van Cliburn Foundation in Fort Worth, Texas, The Dallas Opera, San Francisco Opera, and the Goodwill Arts Festival in Seattle.

Patrons of the two-day event enjoyed not only the outstanding jazz artists who entertained on the Auditorium stage, introduced by veteran jazz

radio personality, Chuck Niles of KLON-FM, but also a variety of gourmet food and drink offered on Ambassador's Fountain Mall. The refreshments were served during a 75-minute dinner intermission on Sunday and were provided by Pasadena restaurants Mi Piace, Parkway Grill and Roxxi, and by San Antonio Winery and Madalena's Restaurant of Los Angeles. Al fresco diners, seated at picnic tables and on the lawns, were treated to the contemporary bebop sounds of guitarist John Snowell and his trio, who performed on a specially constructed stage at the mall during dinner. Displayed on the premises throughout the weekend were three Lexus automobiles, the new SC 400 and the LS 400.

Lexus' sponsorship extends beyond the inaugural Pasadena Jazz Weekend to include Ambassador's entire 1991-92 Sounds of Genius series, which opened on October 9, with jazz saxist Branford Marsalis' Trio. Still to come on Sounds of Genius are the Eddie Daniels Quartet (January 16), George Shearing (February 19), Herbie Mann and his Jasil Brazz Quintet (March 26) and the Stephane Grappelli Trio (May 6). We hope you'll join us for all these events and would like to thank Lexus again for its generous support of Jazz at Ambassador.

Dizzy and the Harper Brothers met for the first time at the August 25 event. Impressed with the Harpers' performance, Dizzy paid them the ultimate tribute: "Our music is in good hands."

PASADENA JAZZ WEEKEND

Photos top to bottom:
Claude Bolling accompanying his Big Band;
Dizzy Gillespie flanked by Philip and Winard Harper;
Poncho Sanchez on the congas;
Ambassador Foundation Vice President, David Hulme, presenting a check to Mr. Richard French of the American Cancer Society as Lexus representative Brett Klein looks on.

2   3

Even long headlines can be quite readable. This sans serif font is very legible and friendly. Making the type big and running it across two columns also aids legibility; such a long headline would have looked cramped and been hard to read at any size if run across only one column. Notice that the subhead under the head on the right-hand page has been set in a serif italic font that contrasts nicely with the sans serif head.

ANSWERING THE COST-ENROLLMENT SQUEEZE:

HIGHER EDUCATION TURNS TO HIGHER TECHNOLOGY

BY CONNIE WINKLER

12

Headlines set in all caps can be somewhat difficult to read, but the use of open letter and line spacing keeps this one legible. The distinctive font has a collegiate feel that is appropriate to the subject.

The Magic Kingdom
by Thane Maynard

Stretching around the earth like an emerald necklace, where the equator crosses Africa, Asia and South America, rain forests remain the tallest, most dense and diverse forests in the world. They are the celebration of life....

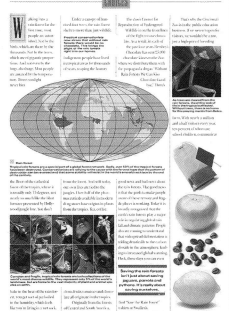

The upper- and lowercase headline is set in a fairly small type size for this large spread, but it's still the first element the eye goes to. Its position inside a pale green tint box surprinted on the very textural photo commands your attention. The initial cap set in the same typeface as the headline and placed in a similar tint box helps direct the reader from the headline into the copy.

7

Subheads

Getting people to read a piece is like fishing. First you catch their attention with some attractive bait (headline and visuals), then you have to hook them (with subheads) in order to pull them into the rest of the copy. Subheads hook readers by expanding on and explaining the headline in an intriguing way. Readers want to know what a piece is about to decide whether they want to take the time and trouble to read the copy. Subheads make it easy to scan an article and learn what it's about.

Subheads also break up a large block of copy into smaller pieces. This reduces the overall grayness of a page, opening it up with more white areas. Breaking the text into smaller chunks makes readers feel that it will be quick and easy to read.

There are many ways to set subheads off from text, but there are some basic guidelines you should follow. Always link subheads visually to the text they introduce so it's clear what goes together. Avoid isolating subheads near column bottoms where they'll be buried and break the reader's concentration.

Don't give readers so many visual clues that you overwhelm them. Tie the design of the subheads to the type treatments of other elements on the page, especially headlines and body copy. It is generally preferable to set the first line following a subhead flush left, especially if the subhead itself is set centered or flush right, to reduce the number of visual breaks and better link subhead and copy.

With Passion and Imagination, Design Holds a Place in the Future
Michael Vanderbyl

Graphic design has been recognized as a discipline and a profession for only a few decades— unlike law, medicine or architecture, disciplines which also straddle the borders of science and art. So, asked to forecast the future of graphic design, one has less precedent and fewer premises to go on. As a designer, I hope to claim a talent for seeing, but not for clairvoyance, and I find that only one or two things in life are inevitable.

The rapid and radical transformations in our culture and in the arts, and the acceleration of the rate of change, make forecasting on the basis of past performance or current trends a hazardous undertaking. There's always a wild card. A personality of tremendous will and vision—a Duchamp or a Mies Van der Rohe—coming out of nowhere and turning things upside down or inside out.

Rules *were* made to be broken. Technological innovations like printing, photography or computer graphics appear and change the production of art or the practice and principles of design forever. Who could have predicted the prismatic perspectives of the cubists or the consequences for architecture of the computer?

"The skills of the graphic designer will take on greater significance in organizing an increasingly complex world."

Understanding the Dialectic of Art and Design
We can look over our shoulder to locate significant turns in the history of art or design. A historical perspective has revealed a dialectic process—the avant garde becomes Old Guard and radical innovation an official institution. We can identify schools and heretics, Blue Periods and Golden Ages; essential differences between the manifestos of Bauhaus and de Stijl and the vernacular expression of the American Arts and Crafts tradition. We can view the social dislocation of the 30s in the activist WPA posters of that decade. Looking at our present decade we can see a strong development of graphic sophistication and a broader application of the principles of graphic design.

With exceptions, graphic design has been perceived as properly two-dimensional, an arrangement of text and images printed upon a page, painted across a wall, posted on a kiosk, decorating a container. Recently, graphic design has stepped off the page and out of the frame as the traditional (and arbitrary) distinctions among architecture, industrial design, and even fashion have been deconstructed (to use a word of the moment).

This crossover between the arts has been as vital to graphics as the ecumenical influence of non-Western cultures. As we all know, architects design chairs and teapots, graphic artists build exhibits and design new patterns for sheets and pillowcases—as well as interactive environments for zoos and children's museums.

Designers in the Service of Business
While the general practice of the graphic arts is not completely new, the ties to commerce and the businessman's new appreciation of the power of graphic translation has given the profession license for wider-ranging activity. Few artists, painters, sculptors or designers have had the luxury of complete autonomy. We have always answered to a patron, a Pope, a client, as well as to the public and our private artistic conscience.

During the previous decade the designer often served under the marketing gurus—the MBAs who based design decisions on the consensus of a focus group or the results of a demographic survey. Unfortunately for design, and ultimately for business as well, this resulted in acceptable rather than exceptional design—typically slick brochures, familiar packaging and "safe" products. We had flash without style, newness without originality, gadgets and gimmicks.

Twenty years ago, designers were assigned the task of devising logos and letterhead, while the marketing department assembled an ad campaign and an architect was commissioned to build a corporate headquarters. This piecemeal approach has been superseded by an orchestrated program—often focused by the direction of a graphic designer. Clients now understand, more than ever before, that design can clarify the purpose and values of the company, reinforce corporate philosophy and define a product's function.

The designer uses space, form, color, material and method to make the client's message tangible and legible through imaginative graphic translation. I would even claim that the graphic designer is uniquely equipped to address each of these elements because all experience is interpretation and every product a symbol and a sign. The graphic artist directs the interpretation of signs.

Thirty years ago, the public heard that the "medium is the message." Cool or hot. And the finest graphic designers have inscribed their messages in a variety of media. Paul Rand, Saul Bass and Milton Glaser applied their artistry to film and airplanes as well as posters and annual reports. Innovative companies like Knoll understood that every product is a graphic, and manufacturing collaborated with design—with designers Vignelli and Sottsass—to produce chairs that have become as "classic" as Ionian pillars.

Knoll recognized that design was the tool to refine their products down to precise detail; designers developed and supported the company's stringent criteria of quality. Design was not a decoration in the service of sales, a way of dressing up the product in order to make it presentable. The uncompromising intelligence of Knoll's designers contributed in the most fundamental way to the success of the company, while the expression of the individual designer in uniquely beautiful products delighted the public.

On the whole, I believe that the tie with business has been good for the profession. The demands of industry can inspire designers to come up with extraordinary solutions, ones that convince *and* delight. The pressure of designing within the confines of commercial necessity can produce the most highly focused and exciting work.

I would like to see designers take more chances. The past few years have been marked by a cynical sophistication, and the drive to achieve seems to be fueled by mercenary concerns. We must not become too businesslike. Perhaps there will be a revival of idealism and even naivete—not affected, but authentic.

The romantic exuberance of the 60s blew the lid off the monotony of high modernism. And perhaps the 90s will soften our hard edge with a new lyricism. A sense of play and of passion. Surprise, humor and the assertion of individual vision. Graphic design is, after all, an expressive art, not simply the perfect execution of technique (not heartfelt but sloppy) but ideally, the expression of a passionate virtuosity.

A Broader Role Demands More Responsibility
As designers take on a greater authority and a broader role as consultants, we also take on greater responsibility. We need to clarify the integrity required of the designer, our responsibility to do honest and artful work. Designers will be held accountable as professionals engaged with the public, with an impact in the moral as well as the economic sphere. Graphic design has become the public's art.

Design informs everyday life in the same way that frescoes and sculpture, mosaic and tapestry informed daily life during the Renaissance. Today those "fine arts" are sequestered in museums or limited to the galleries and public buildings of major cities, and to the private collections of corporations and collectors. The fine arts are physically inaccessible to most of the public and aesthetically inaccessible as well. The public can no longer "see" a painting because it lacks a critical education and the interpretive key of theory. Paintings are esoteric puzzles for an elite clique of other artists and critics.

The world, however, is saturated with images that compete for our attention. They are a major factor in our daily environment and thus their quality has a major impact on the quality of our lives. Until now, architects seemed to upstage graphic and industrial designers, and certainly the urban towers and suburban office parks are crucial influences. In this age of icons and information, however, I believe that the many-faceted, informative skills of the graphic designer will take on increasing significance in organizing an increasingly complex world.

And whether we're designing with pencils on paper napkins or drawing with a mouse on a Macintosh (and I still feel that computers are an aid to tactile design, not a replacement), it is our human experience—our passion and our imagination—that makes graphic design more than visual engineering. That's what makes it interesting. It's the flaws, the accidents, the idiosyncrasies that reveal style and individuality. From graphic designers we can expect the unexpected and hope that we succeed in informing, educating, criticizing and delighting.

Founder of Vanderbyl Design, located in San Francisco, Michael Vanderbyl is also Dean of the School of Design at the California College of Arts and Crafts. Under his direction, Vanderbyl Design has pursued a multi-disciplined course to include graphics, packaging, signage, interiors, showrooms, furniture, textiles, and fashion apparel. Mr. Vanderbyl's line of Esprit home textiles was selected by TIME magazine for its "Best of 87" Design Issue.

AIGA in Chicago/Spring 1990   3

A simple, but effective, type change is all that's needed here to set the subheads off from the copy that follows them. Because there is a strong contrast between the heavy sans serif subheads and the body copy, there was no need for extra line spacing between subhead and following copy or even for a change of type size.

To set subheads off from copy:

• Use a contrasting typeface—a combination of sans serif subhead and serif body copy is generally quite effective. (Try pairing *Futura Condensed* or *Franklin Gothic* with *Times Roman*, for example.)

• Change the type style or size. (For subheads, try using your body copy face in bold or italic or increasing its size by 1 to 3 points.)

• Use a different typeface in a different size for subheads. (Try repeating your headline face in a smaller size that is still slightly larger than the body copy.)

• Align the subhead type differently. (Try a centered or a flush right alignment.)

• Set subheads as hanging indents. (The subhead extends beyond the left edge of the copy that follows it.)

• Wrap the body copy around the subhead; you may need to break the subhead over two to four lines.

• Run a rule above or below them, or both.

• Put them in a box.

• Use a second color.

• Place them in a separate column beside the following copy.

• Give them a graphic treatment using reversed type, a background or a typographic ornament such as a dingbat above or beside them.

●HI/LO HAS WHAT DO-IT-YOURSELF CONSUMERS NEED

THIRTY-FIVE YEARS' EXPERIENCE. In light of the aftermarket's current dynamics, we have many reasons for optimism about Hi/LO's future. With a 35-year history of retailing success and new capital strength to build upon, Hi/LO has begun adding stores at an accelerated pace.

LARGER INVENTORY. The strengths we bring to the marketplace are considerable. For example, modern consumers and mechanics alike now need suppliers with an increasingly wide selection of parts in stock. Hi/LO has it. Hi/LO stores carry between 20,000 and 23,000 stock keeping units (SKUs), twice the number generally carried by our competitors. An additional 40,000 SKUs are readily available from our distribution center.

NEW AND REMODELED HI/LO STORES ARE BRIGHT, CLEAN AND WELL ORGANIZED. A CUSTOM IN-STORE GRAPHICS PACKAGE MAKES SHOPPING EASIER THAN EVER FOR OUR CUSTOMERS AND COMMUNICATES IMPORTANT SHOPPING INFORMATION THROUGHOUT THE STORE.

EFFICIENT DISTRIBUTION. Deliveries link the distribution center to all Hi/LO stores at least three times weekly. And, to accommodate special needs, parts are shipped to store locations twice a day in the Houston area and daily by overnight delivery to other markets. So, when a customer wants something large or small, for a car that's new or old, Hi/LO offers an excellent chance of finding the right part, at an affordable price, within hours.

THE PARTS EXPERTS. Hi/LO associates have the experience and technical knowledge needed to make informed parts recommendations. In helping their customers, Hi/LO associates are aided by an electronic point-of-sale (POS) system. Hi/LO's "Parts-Finder" not only assists in retrieving items from inventory, it simultaneously provides a list of other parts, tools or accessories useful in completing the project at hand. The system tracks sales and inventory, assures pricing consistency and initiates replenishment orders.

CLEAN, BRIGHT, LARGE STORES. Although Hi/LO stores vary in physical layout, they are consistently bright, clean and well organized. The company has 101 remodeled or new stores and plans to continue remodeling and upgrading its older facilities on an ongoing basis. Hard parts are generally housed behind the service counter and on the mezzanine above. Accessories, chemicals and other maintenance items are displayed on gondolas according to a uniform "plan-o-gram" presentation system.

12

Although the subheads run into the body copy and are approximately the same type size, they still stand out easily because they're set in a different typeface and type style (all caps). The small space between the end of the subhead and the first word of the following copy clearly separates them. How much contrast you create between body and subheads and how you create it should be based on the overall graphic effect you are trying to achieve.

Body Copy

Once you've drawn readers into the body copy, make it easy for them to read. Serif typefaces set in upper- and lowercase are commonly used for body copy. For large amounts of copy they are a better choice than sans serif typeface. Sans serifs lack the strong horizontal flow of serif faces and are difficult to read in long blocks of copy. You can use a sans serif for short blocks of copy, but use shorter line lengths and increase the line spacing. Use only typefaces with distinct characteristics, such as *Berkeley* with its unusual bowls and noticeable serifs, when extended readability is not important.

The word, letter and line spacing of body copy all play crucial roles in readability. Type that's tightly packed into a space is hard to read. Give it plenty of room to breath with appropriate margins and spacing. *Times Roman* requires less room than a round, open face such as *Goudy*, which likes to have extra line spacing and wider margins. However, *Goudy* may be a good choice if you have too little copy to fill a space. If you have a lot of copy to fit into a small space, pick a more condensed face that can handle tighter spacing.

You must look at the x-height (the height of lowercase letters excluding their ascenders and descenders) of a face as well as its width. A face with a tall x-height such as *Futura* needs more space between lines because it takes up more vertical space.

---

ethics counselor, explains the importance of ethical employee behavior: "The same rules that apply to the Bank's business with financial institutions or the public in general apply to its internal dealings. Employees have a responsibility to be fair and honest with the Bank and with each other — to behave ethically in the performance of their duties and in the use of Bank resources."

He continues, "A common trap that employees get caught in is viewing ethical behavior as a matter of degrees. Individuals may view one type of behavior as more ethical than another. It seems to me, however, that behavior is either appropriate or inappropriate. A person can't be just a little bit unethical, nor can someone who is unethical in one situation somehow behave differently when confronted with a more important issue."

Specific employee responsibilities consist of protecting the Bank's assets from loss, theft or misuse;

ployees includes: Bank officers, examiners in the Supervision & Regulation Department, attorneys of the Legal Department, and regulatory and statistical specialists in Economic Research.

To protect these employees from potential conflicts, the Bank requires them to reveal personal and family financial interests, as well as employment and indebtedness information annually by completing several disclosure forms. By revealing this information to the Bank, these employees avoid being placed in assignments where conflicts of interest may result. For example, bank examiners, whose positions require interaction with financial institutions and knowledge of confidential information,

Employee commitment Employees in departments throughout the Bank share this attitude of consciousness, and demonstrate their commitment to the Federal Reserve and the important functions it performs by applying the standards of conduct and principles of business ethics to their day-to-day actions and job responsibilities. In doing so, individuals preserve the long-standing reputation of the Federal Reserve System, and promote its ability to support the financial industry and serve the public interest with integrity and objectivity.

Gram concludes, expressing his willingness to assist employees in understanding their ethical responsibilities: "For most employees, the standards of conduct are not a problem. In certain situations, however, when questions arise, I encourage them to talk to me in order to avoid potential conflicts."

Business Ethics

This nice, sizeable serif body copy with its fairly large, round lowercase letters is easy to read. Ample line spacing makes this copy-heavy page look more inviting. Notice that the heavy value contrast between subheads and body copy allowed the designer to eliminate space between paragraphs. The justified columns also create a nice contrast to the angled visual that interrupts the copy.

She examines you carefully, asking a great many questions to get at the origin of the pain, and sends you home with a bottle of antacid and orders to call her the next day — or sooner, if the discomfort worsens. Despite your concern, she does not refer you to a cardiologist.

This is managed care. Is it quality care?

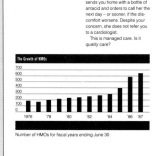

The Growth of HMOs

Number of HMOs for fiscal years ending June 30

Prepaid health plans were born as part of the cooperative movement of the 1930s. It was another forty years, though, before the idea really caught fire, spurred on by the spiraling cost of medical care.

Critics blamed those costs, at least in part, on the fee-for-service system. For decades, patients and insurers had reimbursed physicians for whatever care they provided, regardless of cost. Such a system, the critics said, created more and more care at greater and greater cost — without necessarily leading to better and better health.

for a patient's health. In such a program the patient's care is directed by his or her primary care physician, who acts as the system's "gatekeeper," deciding when tests should be ordered or specialists called in.

Like the old "family doctor," the primary care physician personally handles most of a patient's day-to-day medical needs. But in place of the traditional pay-as-you-go system, the physician in a managed care program receives a pre-determined amount per patient — or in some cases a salary — regardless of how much care he or she actually provides.

Now, in the midst of this rapid growth, many of those involved in health care are pausing to ask some serious questions. What price are we paying for the cost-efficiencies of managed care? Can these plans assure their members of high quality health care? And if so, how should they go about doing it?

"Managed care is here to stay," says Lutheran General Hospital president Roger S. Hunt. "And those of us responsible for caring for patients have to become involved. Above all, we have to see that the mechanisms are in place to ensure that the care provided is quality care."

A Climate of Growing Concern
At its best, managed care embodies many of the principles that the medical world has long advocated but has found difficult to put into practice: continuity of care, comprehensive care and preventive care or "wellness."

Too often, say HMO advocates, traditional health care has meant fragmented, uncoordinated care. Patients move from one specialist to another, their records scattered in half a dozen places, and no one ever sees the total picture. In a managed care program, the patient's medical records are in one location and the primary care physician has all the pieces of the puzzle.

Managed care programs, with their emphasis on cost efficiencies, also have an incentive to keep people well, since prevention is by far the least costly form of treatment. Most managed care

patients of fee-for-service doctors.

Increasingly, however, the press, the public and the medical world are examining the other side of the coin. Among their concerns are these:

– Do the financial incentives of a managed care system lead physicians to withhold legitimate medical care? Do they deny patients necessary surgical procedures or expensive drugs? Restrict access to specialists? Discharge patients from the hospital too quickly?

– Should we accept the limitations on access to specialists and on free choice of physicians that are a part of managed care? Do these limitations pose a risk to members' health?

– Is there a danger in letting someone other than doctors determine where health care dollars should be spent — as is the case when a doctor must get approval to extend a patient's hospital stay?

– What effect will all this have on the doctor-patient relationship? Will it lead to a loss of trust and an intensification of an already litigious atmosphere?

This newsletter shows that sans serif faces can be just as readable as serif faces when handled properly. The nice, round letters and the careful line and letterspacing is clear and legible. The short, staggered columns of copy surrounded by tons of white space invite you to read it.

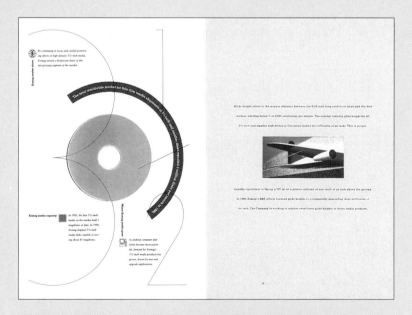

The big body copy set across wide columns with a lot of leading has an open, friendly look that is reflected in the panoramic photo beneath it. Imagine the effect on readers if all the type on the spread had been set small with as many words as possible packed into tight columns. Pretty intimidating, right? Too much, too small is always a major turn off for readers.

Although this copy is set in fairly small type, it is broken into bite-sized chunks with a lot of space around them. This way the reader can quickly and comfortably pick up each bit of information and then move on. The weight and geometric quality of the chosen typeface has a lot of character and even holds up well when reversed while small.

Although every piece has its own personality and its own special typographic needs, there are some type combinations that provide good starting points for working out any layout. Here are some classic combinations for you to use as idea starters:

• *Universe Medium Condensed* for headlines and *Garamond* for body copy

• *Bodoni Bold* for headlines and *Bauer Bodoni* for body copy

• *Caslon 3* set in small caps for headlines and *Caslon* (some suppliers have this as *Caslon 540*) for body copy

• *Gill Sans* for headlines and *Goudy* for body copy

• *Helvetica* for headlines and *Times Roman* for body copy

• *Copperplate* for headlines and *Baskerville* (some suppliers have this as *New Baskerville*) for body copy

• *Palatino Italic* for headlines and *Palatino* for body copy

• *Franklin Gothic* for headlines and *Century Schoolbook* for body copy

• *Helvetica Medium Condensed* for headlines and *Cheltenham* for body copy

• *Futura Medium* for headlines and *Stymie Light* for body copy

Body Copy

Because the designer had a lot of copy to fit in, he chose a legible condensed serif font that let him fit a lot of words per line. Staggering the tops of the columns and using strong graphic elements add interest. Placing the initial cap in a circle clearly signals the beginning of the article to the reader.

The designer took advantage of having little copy to fit, letting it interact with the visual. The large visual and the dramatic, angular white space dominate the page, luring the reader inside the newsletter. A classic serif font suits the period of the play being promoted.

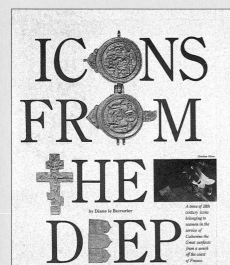

Leading is used here to differentiate the introductory copy from the body of the article. The introduction is set with looser leading than the body copy, which is set fairly tight. This is an effective way to lead the reader into the article. The more loosely leaded copy is easier to read and will propel the now interested reader into the denser copy of the article. As seen in this piece—in which a round, legible serif font has been tightly leaded and a contrast with looser leading established—tight leading doesn't have to give your page an ugly, cramped look.

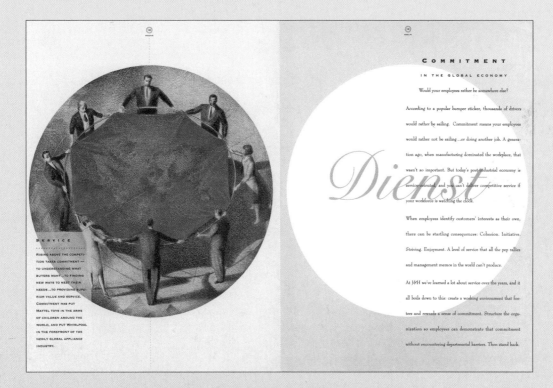

The loose, open leading lets the designer get away with using a smaller, more decorative typeface for this brief copy. The airy look created by ample space around the type helps maintain legibility and readability. Notice the balance of the spread. The circular illustration is mirrored by the circular white shape on the opposite page.

Captions

Good pictures with creatively de-signed captions help persuade browsers to become readers. Pictures and captions show and tell what a piece is about. The pictures show; the captions explain, leading readers to the chosen conclusion. That's why it's important to develop a clear visual relationship between each picture and its caption. The simplest way is to place the caption physically near the picture—above, below or beside it. But many other arrangements are possible as long as readers can match each caption to the right picture.

Captions can be an important graphic element as well. They can contribute as much to creating a lay-out's distinctive look or personality as headlines do. Because captions need to be set off from body copy, they're often set in a bold sans serif or a smaller, italicized version of the body copy's face. Captions can also be set centered or flush right to contrast with body copy set flush left or justi-fied. Their different type design adds contrast and interest to a page.

Sometimes captions are used to break up a page, especially when there is a lot of copy and few pictures to work with. Placing captions in an otherwise empty column adds open space and relieves a gray-looking page besides creating an interesting asymmetrical layout. When there are few other graphic elements in a piece, captions may move up from a supporting to a starring role. Cap-tions can be set in large type with a strong graphic treatment—boxed or set off with rules between each line—in order to break up copy as a subhead, or even another visual, would.

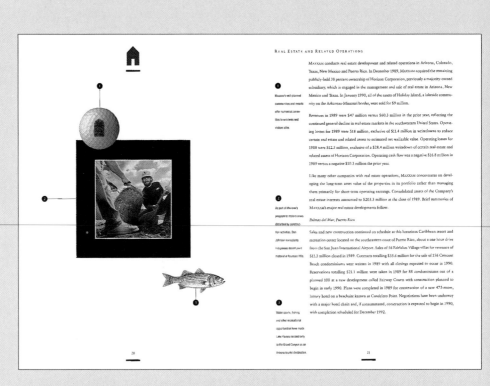

The black, numbered circles link each visual to the appropriate caption, even though the captions are grouped on the opposite page. Grouping the captions kept the page with the visuals open, clear and graphic, which provides visual relief next to the dense page opposite it.

Even though the caption on the right is long, it is clear that it is a caption. The type is set smaller and in a lighter style than the body copy. The columns are narrower. It was made red to tie in to the il-lustration on the facing page and to give it more visual weight and importance.

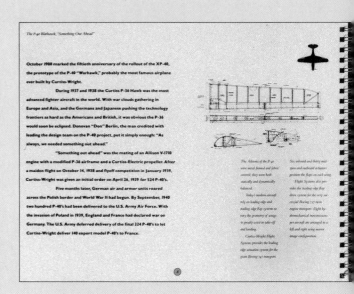

Professor Felton Gibbons, 1929-1990, bequeathed a generous legacy to The Art Museum that will be used to establish an endowment for the conservation of prints and drawings.

Jacopo Palma, called Palma il Giovane
Italian, 1544–1628
Martyrdom of Saint Lawrence
Pen and brown ink over black chalk
21.3 x 20.5 cm.
Gift of Deborah Strom Gibbons,
Graduate School Class of 1979, in honor
of Edward J. Bergman

Professor Gibbons was a member of the faculty of the Department of Art and Archaeology, Princeton University, from 1960 to 1980. He was active in the Museum as assistant director from 1962 to 1964, faculty curator of drawings from 1966 to 1970, and faculty consultant for drawings from 1970 until 1977. A specialist in Italian Renaissance art, he was the author of *Dosso and Battista Dossi, Court Painters at Ferrara* (Princeton, 1968), as well as numerous articles and reviews. In the mid-1960s he was the first to organize small exhibitions in the Museum with an emphasis on drawings to encourage the students in his classes to closely study original works of art.

Last spring the Museum mounted an exhibition of Italian drawings from the permanent collection in honor of Professor Gibbons. On May 18 the family and friends of Felton Gibbons attended a private reception in the Museum to view the exhibition, followed by dinner at Prospect House; three speakers – Jonathan Brown and Robert Bergman, friends and colleagues of Felton Gibbons, and a former student, David Levine, reminisced about Professor Gibbons and paid vivid, personal, and professional tribute to him and to his achievements.

David Gibbons, his son, announced the bequests to The Art Museum and the Department of Art and Archaeology, the latter to assist graduate students. Mrs. Gibbons, Deborah Strom Gibbons (Graduate School Class of 1979), presented a beautiful drawing to the Museum from Professor Gibbons's collection, *The Martyrdom of Saint Laurence* by the sixteenth-century Venetian artist Palma il Giovane, and a very fine addition to the collection.

The Museum is most grateful to Deborah Strom Gibbons and the family of Felton Gibbons for their generosity in providing this occasion and opportunity to honor him. His bequests to The Art Museum and the Department of Art and Archaeology will remain a living tribute to Professor Gibbons and a continuing reminder of his many contributions to the Museum and the tradition of art history at Princeton.

The Art Museum has received a gift of remarkable importance, one that will greatly enrich its holdings of contemporary art. This gift, from Frederick Sommer, consists of thirty color collages and thirty-one black and white photographic renderings, or transformations, of some of these original collages, made by the artist in 1989 and 1990. The group of images, which as a suite was exhibited last year at George Eastman House, Rochester, New York, is titled *Elective Affinities*. The works, a culmination of some fifty years of Sommer's work in collage and photography, are derived from the colored lithographic plates in a nineteenth-century textbook illustrating human anatomy that have been meticulously cut and reassembled. This unique group of works makes Princeton the prime repository for this aspect of Sommer's art.

Frederick Sommer was born in Italy in 1905, and has lived in this country since 1931. A pictorial artist of remarkable sensitivity and breadth, Sommer is considered to be one of the major figures in photography in this century. He is especially representative of the symbolist tradition developed in photography since World War II. He has written on aesthetics and lectured widely and is considered by many to be an artist-philosopher. Sommer's work is already well represented in the Princeton collection with six prints acquired over a number of years, and with four prints in the Minor White Archive. It was Minor White who first published Sommer in depth in 1962 in *Aperture* magazine. Sommer has many personal connections to the University: Emmet Gowin in the Visual Arts Program and Peter Bunnell in The Art Museum; two former Princeton students have been Mr. Sommer's personal assistants in his studio in Prescott, Arizona; and in 1979 Sommer taught at the University as Visiting Senior Fellow of the Council of the Humanities.

Commenting on Mr. Sommer's gift to The Art Museum, Professor Bunnell observed that "the artist, interested in all the arts, and especially impressed with the integration of the photography program at Princeton into the study of the history of art and the active use of the collection in teaching, chose The Art Museum as the repository for these works that so completely blend traditional iconography, concerns for color, arrangement, and form, and for the transforming process of photography. We are deeply indebted to Frederick Sommer for his generosity to the Museum and for his support and encouragement of the program in photography." An exhibition of the entire suite is planned in the near future.

Frederick Sommer
American, born 1905
The Metaphysician, 1990
Collage
30.1 x 35.6 cm.
Gift of the artist

Frederick Sommer
American, born 1905
The Crystal Palace, 1990
Gelatin silver print
27.1 x 34.6 cm.
Gift of the artist

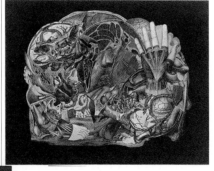

(Above) These captions are simply a smaller version of the body copy's typeface and style. They work because they are set close to the art—whether above, below or beside it. Surrounding the captions with plenty of white space, often placing them in a separate column of the linear grid, helps set them off from surrounding body copy.

There are more ways to handle captions than setting them the same width as your visuals and placing them flush left below them:

• Group them in a paragraph with numbers, colors or symbols to indicate which caption goes with which photo.

• Choose a consistent pica width for all captions (possibly half a column width) and hang captions off of a consistent corner of each visual.

• Run the captions at the end of the body copy with directionals linking photos to captions (i.e., top right, bottom left).

• Use italic type or small caps, one or two point sizes smaller than the body copy, centered under each photo.

• Set each line of a caption within a rule to separate it from the body copy.

• Rag the caption around an outlined image so the image fits into the caption.

• Run all captions in their own separate grid column on the outside right or left of the spread; let them float in white space.

• Set the captions inside a box the same width as the visual and tint the box to match an element in the visual.

• Begin each caption with a slightly larger initial cap.

• Use leading that is much tighter or looser than that of the body copy to set off captions.

• Run the caption in a color. (If small type is used, red will stand out more when the body copy is black.)

Titles

A nameplate (sometimes incorrectly called a masthead, which is generally the listing of staff, address and subscription information) is the title of a newsletter. Unlike a title on a brochure, a nameplate often includes a logo and publication information (issue date, volume and number).

Titles and nameplates are their publications' signatures. Each reflects its publication's personality and is as unique as a person's signature. One of your most important tools for creating that signature is typography.

First, decide what your publication's personality is. Who is the audience? What is your client's image? A piece for a conservative investment firm will look very different from one for a theater.

Then look at the title or nameplate itself. What is the most important word (or words)? Is the title long or short and how much space will it have?

Based on what you know about the client and your layout, choose an appropriate type treatment. Choose a face with the right personality. Script faces can give an elegant, upscale feeling. Serif faces such as *Goudy Old Style* have a dignified air.

Experiment with the type. Make one word lowercase. Try putting a box or a shape around the words. Manipulate the type itself. Wrap it around a graphic or distort it slightly.

This nameplate reaches out and grabs the reader with its strong, dramatic typeface. The great contrast between the huge title and the tiny table of contents copy and visuals lures the reader into exploring further. The motto has been tucked into the white space between the *E* and the *V* and the issue number reversed out of the *W* to add even more interest. This allows the designer to be playful within a fairly rigid format—quite appropriate for a newsletter for the Art Center College of Design.

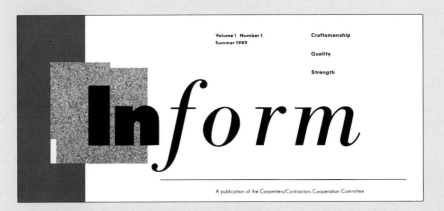

The use of a texture that resembles granite and architectural forms in the nameplate reflects the subject matter, quality and craftsmanship in the construction industry. The contrast of the heavy sans serif, symbolizing strength, with the graceful, italic serif adds an elegant quality that suggests fine architecture. Running the textured box behind the sans serif only adds to the asymmetry of the nameplate and reinforces the feeling of strength.

Pictures can be an important part of a nameplate. Here, the visuals reinforce the name. The blocks of color on either side of the title frame the masthead and give it more weight.

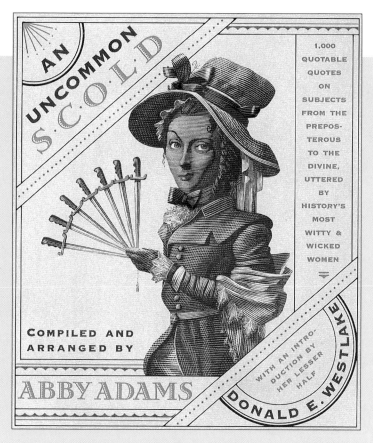

Type becomes a major portion of the visual on this book cover. The cover is divided into unique and varied shapes where little bits of copy are able to tuck inside, yet the copy is still very easy to read. Notice the use of period typefaces for key words like "Scold" and the author's name. The introduction, by popular author Donald Westlake, is given prominence by placing the information in a large circular form.

The type design embodies the feeling of the words. The name of the organization is set straight and very black, standing out against the lighter colored, flowing, more poetic words. Curving the type gives these words a spiritual quality. They almost appear to float on the page, wrapping around the letters YMCA to show all these things are part of the organization.

When designing a title or a nameplate, give it an appropriate personality by choosing a typeface that has a definite character. Here are some ideas for you:

• Use a sans serif or a slab serif typeface like *Helvetica* or *Lubalin* to convey a hard-edged, architectural feel.

• A typeface like *Century Schoolbook*, which is very friendly and easy to read, evokes the feeling of primary education.

• Choose a swirly script like *Snell Roundhand* when you want to communicate a period, nostalgic feel.

• Use a quiet, classic typeface like *Bauer Bodoni* when you want to project an elegant image.

• Select a modern computer-generated face like one from *Emigre* (a type design firm that offers several Macintosh typefaces) when creating a forward looking, youthful feeling.

• Use a face reminiscent of typewriter type, like *Courier,* when suggesting a newspaper-like immediacy.

• *Copperplate*, which resembles hand-set type, suggests craftsmanship and quality.

• Choose a classic serif typeface, such as *Bodoni, Caslon, Century* or *Garamond,* to create an upscale, timeless feeling. You can't go wrong with a classic.

• *Cheltenham Old Style* conveys an accessible attitude and is reminiscent of old alphabet books.

• A bold face like *Futura Extra Bold* suggests a strong, clean, modern quality.

Publication Type

There are many publication elements you can use; several are illustrated here. Which ones you use in a publication will be determined by the kinds and amount of copy you are working with. But no matter how many or how few elements you have, you need to plan how each will look.

Publication elements are road signs directing readers through your piece. If these signs all look alike, readers may not see them or understand what the sign is saying. Think how confusing it would be if "Stop" and "Yield" were on signs with the same shapes. Worse yet, imagine stop signs that looked like signs for street names. Make sure that each element in your publication is distinctive.

You choose how many "signs" your publication will have and how important each one will be. If you introduce too many signals, your readers will get confused and give up on the publication—just as if there weren't enough signals. If you have copy that is split into one main and two related articles, you will need to work with sidebars. If you have only short articles, you won't need, and shouldn't have, jumplines because no articles will be continued over several pages.

Not every publication element has to stand out boldly on the page. A jumpline shouldn't be the first thing readers see on the page. A list should be clearly recognizable as a group of items that belong together, but it should not be so distinct from the rest of the body copy that it's read out of sequence.

tems integrator for computer, hardware, software, communications and technical expertise."

Arnold also said that the recent corporate realignment that established the Bell Group as a strategic business unit, or SBU, has made it easier for Ameritech Applied Technologies to do business with its Bell company partners.

"There was nothing surprising in making the Bell Group an SBU," said Arnold. "That was the direction the company was going. Ameritech Applied Technologies was created to position the Bell Group as an SBU and to integrate its information systems."

The Ameritech Applied Technologies president said, however, that there are still major challenges facing the unit, chief of all being the pressures caused by current budget restraints.

"It looks like 1990 will be more of the same," Arnold said. One positive highlight, he added, was the addition of more than $30 million to the funding of strategic and common systems. "But local has been significantly cut," he stated.

Speaking frankly, Arnold also touched on areas in which Ameritech Applied Technologies fell short of its objectives, but he did not hesitate in sharing the responsibility.

He admitted that upper management sent out conflicting messages concerning the budget. The main reason was that budget circumstances for the entire company changed in

Other achievements Arnold cited included:
• the 1989 baseline study of Ameritech's information processing equipment and capabilities — the first accurate view of its I/T status;
• creation of the first long range I/T plan for the Bell Group;
• completion of the first draft of the Bell Group "Enterprise Model," depicting the major Bell Group business processes and their links to information systems;
• initial development of the Ameritech Intelligent Corporate Network; and
• detailed recommendations for reengineering of major common systems in the Bell Group.

Arnold's "Straight Talk" speech set the tone for the Leadership Conference theme, "leadership and communication."

Though dress was informal for the three-day conference, work was intensive as senior managers attended presentations and workshops designed to help them become more effective leaders.

"Leadership is showing and telling—showing by example and telling what you feel and believe," said Joe Grispo, vice president of customer services and marketing and conference moderator. "Leadership is communication—building teams, gathering information, directing others through your actions and words and sharing your vision."

Since the space between the columns is so small, the bullets for this list are set flush left within the column. The weight of the bullets is not much stronger than that of the type, but it is strong enough to separate one point from the next.

sequence, some critical information may be unavailable on a timely basis to those who need it.

"Recognizing early that the pace of change was accelerating," said Chuck Exley, NCR chairman, "we have prepared to meet the challenge of this new decade we're in. We've developed a strategy to help our customers manage change."

NCR's recent announcement of "Open, Cooperative Computing. The Strategy for Managing Change" sets out a vision of future computing in which data and applications are distributed across a network and can be accessed and shared in a cooperative way, by all authorized users, wherever they are in the network. Open, Cooperative Computing (OCC) will enable organizations to tie together their disparate systems—a complex but achievable task. OCC reflects NCR's long-standing dedication to helping companies turn the challenges posed by changing business environments into opportunities. Open, Cooperative Computing is a natural evolution of developments that have been under way at NCR throughout the last decade. NCR was the first major computer vendor to begin a strategic transition away from proprietary systems with the adoption of an open systems philosophy and the release of the NCR Tower family in the early 1980s. Today, more than half of NCR products are based on open system standards.

"NCR is the first to announce and execute on the concept of open systems computing," states John Dunkle, industry consultant, WorkGroup Technologies. "This NCR effort will do much in setting NCR above the rest of the pack as users enter the '90s."

you need not worry. But if you have made only a few decisions, it's possible that your boss expected too little of you or that you avoided your responsibilities.

• What problems have you overcome? Problem-solving is one of the best ways to make yourself valuable to your company because it shows that you can do something others have not been able to do.

• Have you met or exceeded your objectives? If so, it will reflect positively on your business judgement, your ability to communicate with your boss, and your ability to set realistic goals.

• Are you championing something new? If you have been asked to do so, it shows that you are considered a key player. It also provides a chance to learn new concepts and form valuable relationships.

• Are your skills transferable? Whether you've moved upward in your company or on to another, you need to know how good you are and whether or not your success could be repeated under other circumstances elsewhere.

• Does your performance stand out? You must contribute to the team while making your own performance stand out. If you've moved beyond your peers, it's important to become part of a stronger group. If your performance ranks low among your associates, do something about it.

Change is becoming the norm for organizations of the '90s. Companies are thus developing fluid structures that can be modified as changing business conditions dictate. As future members of these structures, you too will need to devise methods for mastering these changes.

NCR is working to implement career development

that is designed to: promote development and performance, enhance communication, and promote a shared responsibility between individuals and managers.

Although it is perfectly normal to be unsettled by the prospect of an ever-changing work environment, you must recognize that change is normal. If managed properly, change can result in unique growth opportunities for you. It can also be exciting and fun!

Changes in corporate direction can lead to unique career opportunities.

THE 1990s
• Far more individuals will report to each manager.
• Overseas duty will be vital to an executive's advancement.
• Jobs will grow faster than the labor force (below).

Jeremy Main recently reported in FORTUNE: "Now that virtually all the baby-boomers hold jobs, growth of the work force will slow way down—from 2.4% a year in the 1980s to 1.2% in the 1990s. The Bureau of Labor Statistics estimates that the number

These bullets are actually smaller than the copy in the list. However, they are set bold followed by a bold lead-in and treated as hanging indents, which makes them stand out. The rules between the columns establish a clean break that lets the designer hang the bullets without disrupting the smooth flow of the type.

There are many different elements you can use to make your publications interesting:

• The kicker is a summary phrase above the headline that leads readers into an article; if the summary phrase falls below the headline, it's called a deck.

• A lead-in is created by setting the first words of copy in italic, boldface, all caps or a contrasting typeface.

• A header (or running head) is recurring copy at the top of a page—while a footer (also called a footline or running feet) fulfills the same role at the bottom.

• Folios are the page numbers; right-hand pages are odd numbers, while left-hand pages are even numbers.

• Jumplines tell readers where articles are continued from one page to another ("Continued on page 4").

• Sidebars provide supportive material and align related stories.

• Pull quotes, also called breakouts or callouts (also copy tied to parts of an illustration with rules), are brief quotations pulled from the body copy to catch the reader's attention.

• Excerpts or extracts are lengthy quotes taken from another source; they should be set across a narrower column and in a smaller type size.

• A mortise is type in a box completely surrounded by an image.

• The table of contents is more than a listing of the items and their locations (page numbers)—it guides the readers and encourages them to explore.

Publication Type

Plan

As we all know, to reach a goal you need a plan

Customer Satisfaction Through Total Quality... We take customer satisfaction personally... Malcolm Baldrige National Quality Award... Jack Poole Award for Quality... Are they just a bunch of words about the "theme of the month" or is there really something to this quality idea?

According to Jack Poole, vice president/group executive, U.S. Group, "Our goal in USG is to make our quality programs the best in the world in the eyes of our customers, our competitors and ourselves."

As we all know, to reach a goal you need a plan. Business priorities have been set within USG to help meet this goal. They are to become a company totally committed to quality, to strive for an operating style and behavior focused on delighting our customers, and to realize that our employees are the only lasting asset in our business

These goals and priorities are guided by a set of quality policies and principles that provide us a structure in which to operate the business (see side bar, next page.)

In addition to this set of policies and practices, we have an approach to help us get there. That approach is the business strategic long-range plan and the annual business plan that is developed and enhanced on an ongoing basis. Our strategic long-range plan and our annual plan provide at a high level our vision and direction. From this vision and direction, we create strategy and structure and then the implementation steps that we follow on an annual basis.

Sounds good on paper, but how do we know if we're going about things the right way?

The Jack Poole Award for Quality (JPAQ) is the overall tool that we use to check on our progress. It's used to check on customer satisfaction measurements, employee effectiveness and our business results.

There are four key words to keep in mind when looking at our quality process — plan, do, check and act. The "check" part is JPAQ. "When we do a JPAQ report," said Jay Walsh, executive assistant, U.S. Group Executive Office, "what we are doing is documenting the approach, deployment and results of the action items that we have deemed essential in making our business plan. It's a pretty simple thing."

We also have checks such as the Customer Satisfaction Measurement, the Employee Effectiveness Survey and of course our business results. In the final analysis, these are the measures by which the effectiveness of our approach and deployment of what we're doing is gauged. From this process of evaluation, we can discover opportunities to act on to keep ourselves on course. Then the plan-do-act process is continued on an ongoing cyclical basis.

The check stage is an important stage because if we don't take a close look at what we are doing to either verify that it's the right thing to do or discover something that needs changed than the rest of the cycle would be off course. That leads us to take a closer look at JPAQ.

We conduct JPAQ annually to improve our competitive position and to improve sales profit and

Check

revenue. But the number one reason is to achieve worldclass customer satisfaction. In 1992, each division completed an application describing seven key areas — leadership, information and analysis, strategic quality planning, human resource development and management, management of process quality, quality and operational results, and customer focus and satisfaction. Each divisions' application was then reviewed by an evaluation team made up of quality consultants from each division. The home office quality consultants evaluated the field division applications and the field division quality consultants evaluated the home office division applications.

Once the evaluations against the JPAQ criteria were completed, a set of site visit questions were generated for each division. Divisions were then scored on how well they provided clarification on the questions raised by the evaluation team.

In 1992, the JPAQ criteria was altered to mirror the Malcolm Baldrige Award for Quality criteria and features two types of awards: the first for improvement over the prior year and the second for achieving a score against the 1992 guidelines.

The 1992 criteria is based on 1,000 points versus the 500 points used in 1991. The improvement awards include the bronze award, for improvement of 50 or more points on an annual basis; the silver, for improvement of 100 or more points; and the gold, for improvement of 150 or more points. The achievement awards are based on the actual criteria used within the Malcolm Baldrige National Quality Award, beginning with the brass award for a score of 400 to 599 points. Because the bar on the point criteria was raised, there were no gold winners this year.

The winners of the 1992 Silver Improvement Award were the Mideastern Division and the Data Services Division. Bronze Improvement Awards went to the Northern Division, the Western Division, CIMEG and the Financial Systems Division. Two Bronze Achievement Awards were also awarded. These went to the Northern Division and the Customer Services Division.

The winners were announced and presented with their awards at the 1993 USG Kick-Off Meeting in January.

Now that the check phase is complete, we can begin to "act." We can accelerate improvement

through cross-unit sharing. As a by-product of the 1992 JPAQ a "best practices report" is being created.

"We have taken the 28 areas of measurement from JPAQ," said Walsh, "and we've taken those divisions that scored the highest in each area and compiled that into a report. Each division will receive a copy of the report so that they can look at their peers and see who has done the best job of putting programs together — and then implement those ideas in their division. That way we have the leverage of the whole organization."

In addition to the "best practices report" each division received a feedback report which included information on their strengths and areas for improvement.

As a Group, we've made progress, but our rate is slow. We've had obstacles to overcome with the mergers of AT&T/CS and Teradata, but now that the mergers are behind us, additional time needs to be committed to quality. Poole has set three initiatives for 1993: management leadership, make time for quality, and involve everyone in the organization in quality. Quality will be a part of every 1993 program.

Now that the check phase is complete, we can begin to "act"

Act

"With a dedication to quality," said Poole, "we can position customer satisfaction as a strategic weapon. If we do this, we will be recognized as the company known for customer satisfaction in our industry."

Our Quality Policies are to:
- Consistently provide products and services that meet or exceed the quality expectations of our customers
- Actively pursue ever-improving quality through programs that enable each employee to do his or her job right the first time
- Continuously foster strong quality awareness among USG people

Our Quality Principles are:
- The customer comes first
- Quality happens through people
- All work is part of a process that can be continuously improved
- Suppliers are an integral part of our business and should subscribe to the same quality standards
- Prevention is achieved through planning, and
- Quality improvement never ends

The sidebar has a different typeface than that of the body copy, but the weight and size of the type is the same. The change from serif body copy to sans serif sidebar copy visually reinforces the fact that the sidebar contains separate information from the body copy.

The circular treatment of the breakout provides a nice contrast to the boxy, justified body copy. Its asymmetrical placement also helps to draw attention to it at a glance. Even though the centered callout is set in a small and elegant typeface, the half circle of space surrounding it calls attention to it. The reader will be drawn to it and then into the copy to find the context of the quote.

Don Wolf, *General Atlantic Resources:* I had initially worked with an individual investor. But in GA I found greater depth and breadth — they just had more financial experience, with a broader variety of transactions, and a wider knowledge of company building than, I think, the average individual investor has. A lot of the benefit that General Atlantic brings has to do with that breadth of experience, and the great exposure they have to numerous transactions, economic analyses, and deal structures. All this gives them a perspective on company direction, on certain keys to building value, that people who aren't in a high-volume, deal-flow environment just don't get exposed to.

Michael Cline, *Vice President, General Atlantic:* I believe we are able to add value consistently because we take a very concentrated approach. We work within a limited number of industries, and we put a lot of money into a smaller number of companies. By doing this we can spend real time with each company. And I think you are better able to add value to a business if you understand the industry within which it operates and spend the time to understand the issues the business faces.

LONG-TERM VIEW

Steve Reynolds, *General Partner, General Atlantic:* Because of the source of our capital, we can take a long-term approach. That gives us a tremendous advantage, in that we are able to encourage our companies to focus on building long-term value rather than short-term gain. We have a fundamental conviction that if you build for the long term it actually gives you more options in the short term.

Jeff Sandefer, *Sandefer Oil and Gas:* These days, people do a lot of deals just for the sake of doing them. The General Atlantic people aren't like that. They pick an industry and go very deeply into it — until they understand every facet, all its cycles and all its people. And the result of that deep understanding is that they don't spook at the first downturn.

LONG-TERM APPROACH

"WE ARE ABLE TO ENCOURAGE OUR COMPANIES TO FOCUS ON BUILDING LONG-TERM VALUE RATHER THAN SHORT-TERM GAIN."

HARRY CALLAHAN
Morocco, 1981

HAMON ARTS LIBRARY

The Hamon is one of the most technologically advanced libraries in the country. Sophisticated security and environmental systems protect the Hamon's collections for future generations. Audio and video materials, from cylinder recordings to the latest compact and video discs, as well as powerful music and graphic computer workstations are available. Almost all of the 50 public access computers planned for the Library will be interconnected through a local area network offering building directories, tutorials and other resources. Students and faculty now have the opportunity to familiarize themselves with technologies which will be *de rigueur* for professional artists and scholars in the twenty-first century.

In addition to information on the arts, the Hamon offers a regular schedule of exhibits in the Mildred Hawn Exhibition Gallery. The Gallery has already featured two exhibitions based on materials in the Jerry Bywaters Collection, and the first in a series of didactic exhibits on the research value of different types of library materials (*The Art of the Facsimile*) opened in April.

Recent acquisitions to the Jake and Nancy Hamon Arts Library include works of art (Dallas artist Malcolm Furlow presented a portrait of Indian Chief Quanah Parker in December), more than a thousand books (ranging from volumes on Mexican art to a specialized collection on dance injuries), and archival items documenting Southwestern art for our special collections. To the hundreds who have given library materials, funds, or time, we express our appreciation.

Every important library is comprised of four critical elements: adequate space and equipment, strong and growing collections, timely access to information regardless of where on the earth it resides, and sufficient staff to empower library patrons in their use of the Library. With the Hamon, we have one of the finest physical facilities in the country. We look forward to the challenge of building collections, access, and staff of equal distinction.
Robert Skinner, Head, Hamon Arts Library

"The play of light between the screen wall and the facade is particularly intriguing, and at night the building takes on an inviting glow."
David Dillon

"When the adjacent Greer Garson Theatre (also by Mr. Powell) opens in 1992, SMU will have two new buildings with architectural energy and considerable public presence."
David Dillon

Paul Talley

Doug Hopler

John Veuer/kamuder

"...this main link (Taubman Atrium) to the Meadows building is a space that counts for something instead of being just a utilitarian corridor. It gives the entire complex a celebratory feel that it has lacked."
David Dillon

John Vueuer/kamuder

View of the Garson Theatre construction site looking south to the Jake and Nancy Hamon Arts Library.

The Jake and Nancy Hamon Arts Library houses several important collections comprised of original works of art, manuscripts, letters, photographs, and archival materials in theater, art, music, film, and dance. The Jerry Bywaters Special Collections Wing, which was made possible by a generous gift from the McDermott Foundation, protects 100,000 rare, fragile, or valuable items in a secure and environmentally controlled vault and provides a study room for researchers to use materials and work space for curators to process them.

Chief among our holdings are the Jerry Bywaters Collection on Art of the Southwest, the McCord/Renshaw Theater Collection, and the Paul and Viola van Katwijk Music Collection. The Bywaters Collection comprises one of the most extensive collections in the United States of archival material concerning the art of the Southwest. Jerry Bywaters, Professor of Art at SMU from 1938 to 1970 and former director of the Dallas Museum of Fine Arts, assembled the nucleus of this collection. Beginning in the late 1920s, and extending over the next six decades of his career as an artist, critic, curator, and teacher, Professor Bywaters amassed catalogs, clipping files, correspondence, photographs, and works of art on paper. He donated this approximately 130 linear feet of archival material to SMU at intervals from 1980 until his death in 1989. While the Collection's main focus is on Texas and the Southwest, its holdings also include supporting material on American, European, Mexican, and ethnic art. More than 700 files are devoted to individual artists and architects and some 300 folders are organized according to specific museums, galleries, organizations, and collectors. In addition to its archival holdings, the Collection has an ongoing oral history project of interviewing artists and art professionals, with tapes and transcriptions available for researchers.

The McCord/Renshaw Theater Collection, since its inception in 1933, has had as its central purpose the acquisition and preservation of papers, playbills, photographs and other materials related to all the performing arts. The Collection is named after Professor Mary McCord, a pioneer teacher and director of theater at SMU, and Dr. Edyth Renshaw, a student of Professor McCord and long-time SMU faculty member who oversaw the growth of the Collection. The Collection's holdings, approximately 250 linear feet of archival materials, emphasize the performing arts in Texas and the Southwest, including papers of the Dallas Little Theatre and SMU's Arden Club.

Jerry Bywaters' mural design submitted in competition for lobby of Dallas Post Office Terminal Annex, 1938 (detail).

John Vueuer/kamuder

"The most compelling spaces on the main floors are the semicircular reading rooms. These are comfortable, unpretentious spaces designed with the pleasures of curling up with a good book in mind. The curve of the wall is repeated in the furniture, the balconies and the detail of the recital hall, an architectural leitmotif that helps to pull the building together visually."
David Dillon

The Paul and Viola van Katwijk Collection was donated by Mrs. van Katwijk, an accomplished pianist and composer, over the course of several years, beginning in 1974. Her husband, Dr. Paul van Katwijk, was associated with SMU from 1918 to 1955, serving as Dean of Music and as head of the piano department. He also served as conductor of the Dallas Symphony from 1925 to 1936. The Collection consists of over 500 monographs of music, 1400 scores, 100 concert programs (with related materials from Europe and America), and a number of photographs and other memorabilia documenting musical life in Dallas. Of special value are the manuscripts and printed compositions of the van Katwijks (three linear feet) and archival materials related to their lives and careers (twelve linear feet). Also of considerable importance is their collection of over 100 autographed letters and manuscripts, many of well-known composers and musicians, including Debussy, Mahler, Rachmaninov, Rossini, and others.

Special Collections is open weekdays from 8:30 a.m. - 5 p.m. Researchers are requested to make reservations in advance whenever possible so that the required materials can be assembled and the appropriate curator made available.
Dr. Sam Ratcliffe ('74), Head, Special Collections

Boxed sidebars don't have to be squares or rectangles. The stairstep shape of the sidebars adds visual interest to the spread and attractively frames the central body copy. The orange tint of the sidebars further sets them off from the copy and adds a playful quality to the spread.

Ad/Display Type

Ad and display type offer great opportunities for typographic creativity. Most rules about how to treat type are now meant to be broken. Proper names are set without caps, and opening paragraphs are set all caps. Even reading from left to right is abandoned. Words can run vertically or diagonally or be read backwards. You can play with type the same way an illustrator manipulates imagery.

Display type is generally large (18 point or larger). Letterforms may be strong and simple or complex and decorative. Words are treated in a visually arresting way, as has been done with the Sinead O'Connor article opener on page 26. The treatment you choose must match the look of the piece. This is especially important since display type often dominates a piece due to its size. Your display type should also be appropriate for your readers. Conservative lawyers won't show much interest in an ad with wild, funky display type.

Advertising type is used to set body copy in ads. You can take more liberties with it than is usually the case with body copy. Although readability is still important, tight word and letterspacing are often used to fit copy into small spaces. When you must pack type, choose a face that is comfortable with little white space. You can also tighten leading to save space.

These ads are simple yet effective. Each headline quickly grabs attention with its heavy sans serif type and the generous amount of white space surrounding it. Running the type vertically rather than horizontally across the top of an ad is unexpected and intriguing. Readers caught by the headlines will be drawn into taking a second look because neither picture matches the word in the headline. The gentle humor gives the ads their whimsical charm.

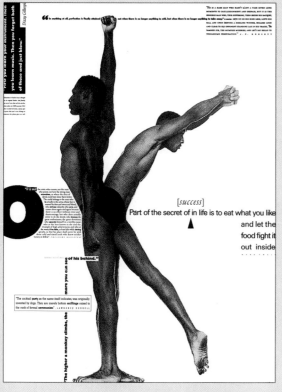

It's amazing how much excitement and variety you can create simply by playing with type. The designer of these posters has made the type part of the illustration rather than separating the two elements. The type works around and into the images, challenging you to explore it, as it demonstrates the many ways typography communicates. Some type is set large, bold or reversed to shout, while other, very small, delicate blocks of copy whisper. The type races vertically, horizontally, even diagonally, demanding attention as it creates positive and negative shapes.

When working with display type:

• Remember that some display faces only look good in large sizes (*Balloon*, like the toy it's named for, looks best when blown up large, while *Bodoni Poster* works well when used either large or small).

• Be aware that display type can be made from some body copy faces but not others (*Times Roman* and *Garamond* perform both roles well, while *Palatino* doesn't).

• Always kern the type manually to achieve the correct letterspacing.

• Superimpose type on a visual only if there is an empty or very light area large enough to hold the headline; if there's not enough contrast, the type will be too hard to read.

• Don't set long blocks or large areas of display type reversed; it becomes too hard to read.

• If setting more than one line, make sure the space between the lines looks equal (it may have to be unequal to look right)—if it looks right, it is right.

• Remember that type set both upper- and lowercase is easier to read than all caps (if you need all caps for a particular effect, take extra care with spacing).

• Don't set type large *and* bold because it looks horsey—everything gets heavier as it gets larger (if you need large, bold type for an effect, give it plenty of space).

• Know that rules are made to be broken—but only when you understand and can apply the rules well.

Ad/Display Type

ICEBOX Custom Framing

Picture Framing Studio And Gallery, 2401 Central Avenue, Northeast Minneapolis, 612.788.1790.

Because of the strength of the image, very little copy is needed to catch the reader's attention. The visual was photographed so the hand holding the frame is thrust into the image being framed. This makes it appear that the ad's reader is the one holding the frame. When there is little copy, you can use more distinctive typefaces and give the ad more white space, as was done here. Surrounding the type with the extra white space helps call it to the reader's attention even though it is only a small portion of the ad.

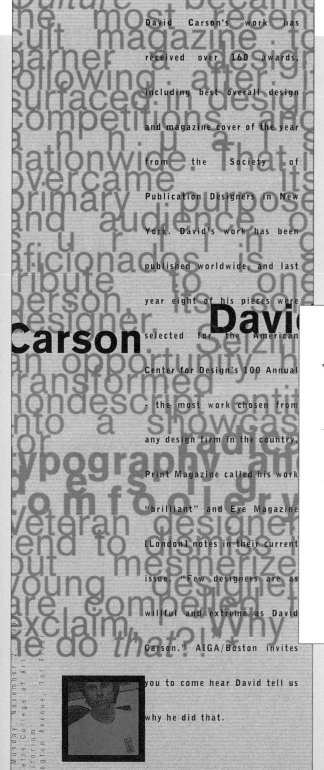

Type becomes texture on the poster/announcement at right. The color and size changes create just enough contrast among the different typographic layers for readers to comprehend the message. Even with all the activity, the first words you read are "David Carson," the subject of the piece. Notice that the date, time and place information are made extremely legible and barly overlap any other type.

There is a lot of copy in the above ad, but it is broken up with little visuals and a humorous head that cuts right through the copy. The humorous copy is made even more readable by setting it in a very legible serif face with a lot of line spacing. Notice that the designer has saved space for and added interest to the copy by using little G-clefs, a punctuation device (dingbat) closely related to the subject of the ad, to mark the beginning of paragraphs rather than the traditional indents.

Ad/Display Type

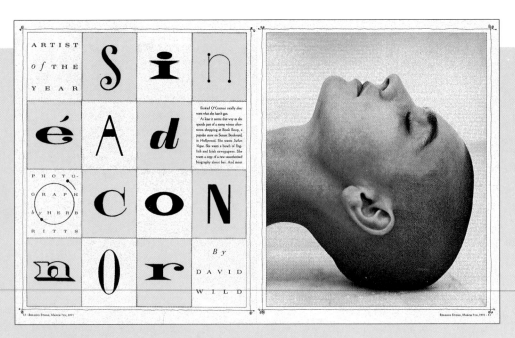

The possibilities for display type are endless. This introductory spread is intentionally challenging to read in order to intrigue and involve the reader. The charming, distinctive typefaces used to set each letter of the headline create an animated contrast to the stark, simple photo.

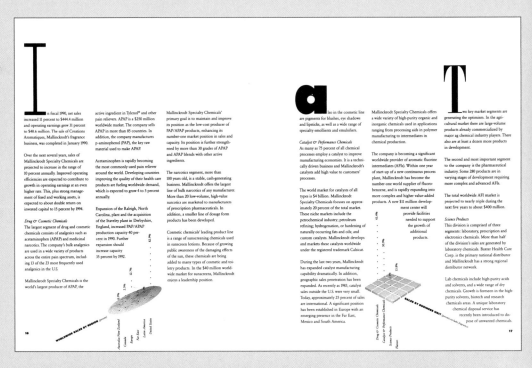

Throughout this annual report, the large initial caps are a strong design element, as well as clear signals for the beginning of each new section of copy. The columns of type always begin on the same baseline, which creates an interesting rhythm with the black letterforms that rise to different heights above them. Changing the typefaces and even condensing or expanding fonts gives this annual report a friendly, lively quality that seems to promise more interesting reading than the average report.

The typography *is* the design in this brochure. The display typeface used on each spread was carefully chosen to relate to the image and the feel of the message. On this spread, the choice of a very classic, chiseled serif face printed on a letterpress reinforces the sense of history and tradition conveyed by the copy. Running the smaller type between each line of display type allows the designer to convey two thoughts simultaneously. Because of the vast difference between the styles and sizes of the two typefaces, the reader can visually separate the two.

"ACTS OF CREATION ARE ORDI-

Aldo Leopold (1887-1948), who once

NARILY RESERVED FOR GODS AND

worked for the U.S. Forest Service, was an

POETS, BUT HUMBLER FOLK MAY

early advocate of wildlife management

CIRCUMVENT THIS RESTRICTION

in America and instrumental in defining

IF THEY KNOW HOW. TO PLANT A

contemporary land ethic. His book,

PINE, FOR EXAMPLE, ONE NEED

"A Sand County Almanac" is considered

BE NEITHER GOD NOR POET;

a classic in environmental literature.

ONE NEED ONLY OWN A SHOVEL."

— *Aldo Leopold, from "A Sand County Almanac"*

IVORY COVER 80 LB.

◄ COMMUNICATION TOOLS ►

Article by

CEO

for Employee Newsletter

22

Many of us who work at *(name of hospital)* are environmentally responsible in our personal lives. We check our cars' emissions, we try not to waste water, we may save newspapers and bottles for recycling – not just because those may be the rules, but because we know it's for a good cause. Some of us go a step further and actively support environmental groups. By what we say and do – and don't do – we are taking a stand on this issue.

(Name of hospital) as an institution must take a stand on the environment, too. There are certain practices we must follow to assure a safe environment for our patients, our employees, and our neighbors. You are familiar with most of them: they include the special handling of waste classified as infectious or hazardous; training employees in occupational safety practices such as disposing of sharp objects; and handling, storing, and disposing of all materials in a way that doesn't hurt the public or the environment. For example *(describe or name present disposal process – incinerator and/or landfill)*.

But I think *(name of hospital)* can do even more. We can choose to go beyond the rules and regulations and become a leader in the environmental movement. If our central concern is preserving the health of our patients and the community, then we should also be concerned about the health of the larger environment they live in.

One thing we can do/are doing is reduce the amount of garbage that we incinerate/send to landfills. From the cafeteria to the mail room to the lab, we can all be more aware of which materials might be reusable and how our work habits affect the environment. We can collect and recycle *(computer paper, newspaper, cardboard, aluminum, plastic, glass . . .) (reword depending on policy of hospital)*. In hospital offices we can give up Styrofoam for reusable cups, use outdated stationery for internal notes, and photocopy on both sides.

We can choose to go beyond the rules and regulations and become a leader in the environmental movement.

Reusing materials and recycling are good for the environment, and they make good sense for the hospital. Not only are we setting a good example in the community, but we are reducing our supply costs and cutting our costs for *(incineration/landfill hauling)*.

Another way *(name of hospital)* can become an advocate for the environment is by educating the public about environmental issues in general, and especially about medical waste. Most people don't know what medical waste is – they're just certain it must be bad. Waste audits show that more than half of hospital waste is paper and cardboard; another third is food waste and food containers, such as tin and aluminum cans. The part that is potentially infectious is carefully separated, as you know, and disposed of safely. There is not a single case of improper disposal of hospital waste causing an infection in the community, according to a survey article in the Journal of the American Medical Association.

But misconceptions about medical waste and the environmental impact of incineration and landfill disposal have caused serious image and community relations problems for some hospitals. We can help *(name of hospital)* avoid such problems by learning more about environmental issues ourselves and by telling our community more about our *(recycling and)* waste disposal efforts. We can also help our community by offering tips on disposing of home health items and reducing household waste. *(Mention brochure if used.)* Every employee can play a part by helping to tell our story and acting as an "environmental ambassador" from the hospital to the community.

To me, the prospect of *(name of hospital)* becoming a leader in the environmental movement is an exciting one. I hope you'll agree, and that you'll join in your own way, both at home and at work.

23

P

reserving the earth's environment is clearly an idea whose time has come. The public's concerns have led McDonald's to give up foam packaging for its hamburgers and supermarkets to recycle their plastic grocery bags. Such changes illustrate that we're beginning to understand that the planet has limited resources, and that thoughtless exploitation has already damaged some of it.

Who wouldn't read at least the opening paragraph and the callout on this spread? The opening paragraph with its large type and heavy initial cap grabs readers and pulls them in. It's friendly rather than overwhelming because it's short and sweet. Readers drawn in by the opening paragraph move quickly through the body of the article, which is surrounded by dotted lines to give it a self-contained, clean feeling.

A Few Last Words

In this chapter, we've shown you many ways to make type an attractive, effective communication tool. However, even outstanding type designs lose most of their effectiveness if the typography is of poor quality. The most beautiful decorative typeface in the world won't attract a reader who can't distinguish one letter from another because the letterspacing is too tight.

Take the time to set proper letterspacing. If letters are too tightly set, the letterforms run together. This makes headlines or copy not only hard to read but also unattractive to look at. If the letters are too loosely set, the readers may abandon the effort to decipher a line of type before they've finished the first paragraph. (Too tight or too loose word spacing poses the same problems for readability and appearance.) Whenever possible, take the time to check the kerning of individual pairs carefully. Fine-tune the kerning of display type if you do nothing else. (When type is enlarged, the kerning becomes uneven and should be adjusted.)

Eliminate rivers (vertical white streaks caused by spaces aligning over four or more lines), widows (created when the last line in a paragraph is shorter than the depth of the paragraph indent on the next line or when the first line of a paragraph stands alone at the bottom of a page or column) or orphans (short fragments of a paragraph appearing at the top of a page or column). Justified type may have large, gaping spaces inserted between words by a computer. When type has been set ragged right, you may end up with an unsightly deep rag that spoils the look of your copy. Odd shapes may also appeared silhouetted along the edge of a block of ragged right copy. Eliminate these with editing or small typographic adjustments.

Proofread any copy thoroughly—even if you know the client will also be proofreading it. Never computer spell check material and quit; a spell checker won't appreciate the difference between "to" and "two." Beware of "typewriter formatting." Typists are taught to put two spaces between sentences; for typesetting you need only one. Inserting multiple spaces in place of tabs is a common bad habit among amateur word processors; if you don't hunt these down, they will stick you with awkward indents that you don't want.

The smart quotes function in your page layout program should convert all the typewriter-style quotation marks to real, "curly" quotes. Some programs, however, have trouble with single quotes inside double quotes or quotes inside parentheses. Dashes can be problems if the typist input them as "space hyphen space" instead of "hyphen hyphen." Your hyphenation function is another potential troublemaker—more than three hyphens in a row looks ugly.

Chapter 2
Pictures

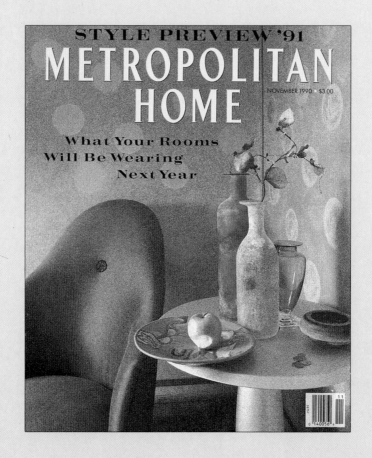

Because visuals communicate your message quickly and memorably, choose and use them with great care. A picture really can be worth a thousand words, but only if it's the right picture. A visual can command individual attention, like a famous sports or movie star, but it must be a team player, too. Every element of a layout must mesh and work together to achieve the planned effect.

When choosing a visual or graphic element for a layout, first consider what you want the element to achieve. Do you need a visual to make an abstract idea concrete? Do you need to reinforce the headline? Do you need a dramatic, emotional image to grab the viewer's attention? Do you need a beautiful image to inspire viewers or to lure them into your piece? Do you need rules, boxes, borders or backgrounds to add interest and organize your material?

Once you know why you're using a visual or other graphic element, decide how and where you'll use it in your layout. Plant visuals strategically—never randomly —so they are perfectly integrated with all the other elements of your layout. Take advantage of the way visuals can attract attention, beautify a layout, add excitement and even provide a resting place for the readers.

This chapter shows how to use visuals and graphics to beautify and communicate.

Type as Art

Type can be transformed into artwork by treating letterforms, words or even blocks of copy as individual pieces of art that can suggest a shape, create texture, communicate a message or mood or become a visual pun. Type used as art can create powerful messages, but its success depends on layouts that spring from the message, the shape of the page or the positioning of the logo, and the number of words involved.

Sometimes you don't need artwork to communicate your message. If a company's name lends itself to a visual typographic treatment, use it as a logotype. Posters promoting organizations that combat illiteracy or learning disorders have used creative typography, not art, to demonstrate reading difficulties.

Turn letterforms into art. Think about the shapes of the individual letters. Do any of them remind you of objects associated with the message of your piece? An *s* could be a seahorse, a snake or the knight from a chess set, depending on your context.

Explore the possibilities of decorating letterforms or complete words. Place an initial cap inside a textured box. Mix type and color for instant impact. Set the letters or words of a headline in alternating colors or type styles to create excitement.

The flowing letterforms of calligraphy can add grace, beauty and elegance to a piece. Hand-drawn lettering can exaggerate the look or personality of a typeface to make it more interesting or appropriate.

This logotype is truly a unique signature. The angularity of the letters suits the name and the personality of the restaurant. Each letter has been carefully designed and drawn with similar characteristics so they create a single, memorable impression of the restaurant. An even more stylized *B* and *G* are combined into a monogram that serves as a separate signature element.

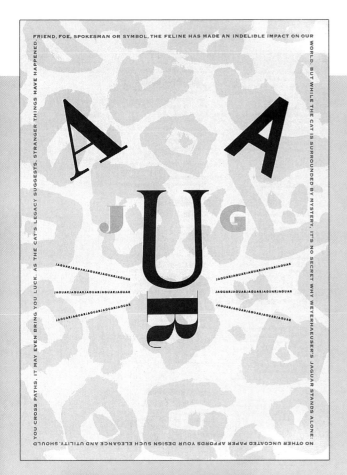

Type can literally become art when letterforms are used to create pictures. Here, the word "Jaguar" becomes a cat face because the designer looked at the shapes of the letters, moved them around, and then enlarged some letters and reduced others to create a symbol of the word.

There are many ways you can turn type into art, here are a few ideas you can try:

• Change type styles or weights within the body of the word.

• Use geometric shapes to suggest letterforms.

• Explode the word across the page.

• Rearrange the letters to create a recognizable picture that fits the word or words.

• Turn letters upside down or on their sides to form the shapes you need in a picture.

• Illustrate around a letter and use it to begin body copy.

• Repeat letterforms to create a texture.

• Contrast huge type with minuscule type.

• Gradate, stretch or condense type to create new styles.

• Mix caps and lowercase letters to develop a rhythm.

The invented word "öola," chosen for its geometric letterforms and the umlaut, has become the central motif in the retail identity for this chain of candy stores. Using the letters to create whimsical faces not only makes the identity easily recognizable but also gives it a friendly personality.

Information Graphics

Charts and graphs clarify information, facilitate understanding and streamline communication. They make it easier for the reader to come to a conclusion quickly. When designing an info graphic, consider what the figures say and then interpret them visually. Select the best tool for the communication job at hand.

Use pie charts to show proportion and percentages. Bar and column charts make it easy to quickly compare several items. Line charts show trends. Graphs show changes against a rectangular grid. You can also combine chart types; a single chart can show not only a company's total sales but also each product's share of those sales over time.

Charts and graphs should attract as well as inform to make those facts and figures easy to digest. Information graphics integrate traditional chart or graph elements with pictorial representations to achieve this goal. Simple, direct illustrations can give the dullest chart a warm, understandable, human face. For example, a pie chart showing the percentages of cookie sales to different outlets might be drawn as a cookie.

You can also illustrate around, behind or beside charts and graphs. You could show a graph of increased cat food sales that appears to be on a cat food box or surround it with a border of playful cats.

Simply arranging complex information in a chart can communicate even a lengthy message quickly. Annual reports have column after column of numbers for readers to wade through. A good chart, like this one with a more traditional design, can help readers easily read and digest difficult material.

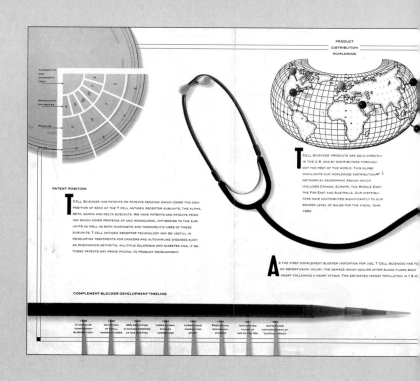

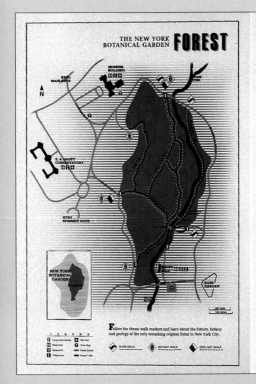

How do you make a map and an introduction to a park interesting? Communicate the information in a lively and memorable way. We understand pictures before words, and pictures retain their power to attract and influence us all our lives. Every bit of copy is reinforced with a visual. The visuals also lead readers from one bit of copy to the next. Info graphics should tell the story with almost no help from the copy. And that's true here. Readers can benefit from the map and sign even if they don't read all the copy.

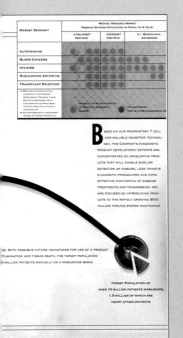

Illustrated charts can become an integral part of a layout. Here the selection of medical products used as visuals matches the chart's subject perfectly. But the visuals aren't just pretty; each reinforces and clarifies the message of the piece. Note also the variety of charts used to convey the message. There are two different pie charts, a timeline, a map and a bar chart.

When designing a chart, graph or diagram:

• Choose the right chart for the job (bar charts make comparisons while line charts show trends).

• Choose diagrams over charts when you want to emphasize relationships and sequences rather than numbers.

• Add impact with size, color or appropriate visuals (use larger and smaller houses to represent changes in the number of houses being built).

• Make sure all type, both words and numerals, is highly legible—a tricky feat when dealing with 7 point type.

• Remember that numerals may need special kerning and spacing for the best legibility.

• Use thin rules or dotted lines between rows or columns of a table for maximum readability.

• Keep the relationship between the labels and the parts of the chart or graph they identify clear and distinct.

• Make a basic line chart look as if it's three-dimensional to add impact to its message.

• Keep tables visually separate from surrounding type to make them easier to find and read.

• Make information easy to find and visually well organized (no one wants to grope through a jungle of bright colors and graphic elements for hours to figure out sales figures).

Graphic Elements

Rules, boxes, borders and backgrounds add interest and color to your design projects. Although graphic elements are decorative, they can assist with the communication on the page—to provide good readability, to control visual flow throughout the material, and to achieve isolation from or integration with items on the page.

Any graphic element may be used to emphasize or frame an item in a layout. Borders can frame the entire live area of an ad or a page. This is especially important when working on ads that appear in busy environments. In brochures and other publications the margins around each page create borders that frame the contents.

Graphic elements are excellent organizational tools when used to isolate or to group items in a layout. Placing a background texture behind a visual and related copy signals the reader that these belong together. Sidebars are often set in boxes to separate them from body copy.

Make sure rules, boxes, borders or backgrounds are appropriate to the theme of your piece. An ornate floral border wouldn't work in a brochure promoting a rustic ski lodge. Keep color and contrast in mind. Thick rules darken a piece and are most effective when set off by ample white space. Look at your page in terms of shades of gray; anything less than 60 percent contrast between two items produces mud. So plan backgrounds and screen tints (10 percent to 20 percent screens are safest) that complement rather than overpower your type.

Imagine this ad without the rules—you couldn't find your way from one end of the copy to the other. The designer has made a ton of information manageable simply by using rules to separate it into sections. Readers can easily move through each section of copy and then act by filling out one or more clearly marked coupons at the bottom. The strong border around the ad not only visually unifies the piece by grouping all the sections together but also sets this full-page ad off from other information in a crowded newspaper.

Working With Words & Pictures

You can use graphic elements to emphasize, frame or separate items by:

• Separating columns of type with thin rules.

• Setting a rule above and below a pull quote to visually separate it from body copy.

• Running a tint box behind a visual and its caption to group them.

• Creating reader-response coupons with boxes made of dashed lines.

• Framing an ad with a striking, appropriate border to set it off from other items on the page.

• Placing a border around several visuals and their captions to group them.

• Surrounding the message area on a sheet of letterhead with a border.

• Dropping type out of a ramp of gradated color (make the type bold for better readability).

• Using the same background on each piece of a unified stationery system.

These borders are primarily decorative, framing the copy and other visuals. In the "Spring Floral Festival" ad, at top, the border is the dominant visual, echoed by the tiny pieces of line art that mark the start of each paragraph of copy. The border for the "Indian Spirit" ad is much less important than the photographs in the ad, yet it adds a nice textural frame. Note also that each border is appropriate to the message and personality of each ad.

Graphic Elements

The triangle at the top of this bag is a functional "box" that calls out and separates the information within it. It allows the consumer to quickly find and extract information about this product. Color, shape and placement all help to signal that this information is important. In a sense, the front of the bag itself has been turned into a "box" framed by the brightly colored sides of the bag.

Boxes demand attention. They clearly separate any special copy—or copy related to but not part of the main article—from the body copy. Here the "Mailbox," a request for queries from readers, is boxed off and set with a warm beige tint because this call to action must get noticed. A call for action, an offer of piano lessons, on the inside spread is highlighted the same way.

EXTERIOR

DECORATING

The secret to outdoor furnishings is in the mix

In the past, outdoor furniture has distinctly reflected the period of its manufacture. Adirondack twig furniture recalls those other '90s; deck chairs bring '30s ocean liners to mind; designers in the '60s discovered European cafe tables.

Today the trend is toward a mix of old and new, elegant and homey. The furniture of several generations coexists in a California backyard: true antiques, reproductions, "homage" pieces and frankly contemporary furniture.

Produced and styled by Jill Sharp-Miller   Photography by Tim Street-Porter

Contemporary handmade twig chair *(this page)* in the Adirondack tradition. California-made cast concrete stepping stones *(facing page, top)* bring a wee thistle to the garden. Aubusson tapestry *(bottom right)* graces this 1937 deck chair by Colett Gueden.

A photograph of twigs becomes a background for this spread. It's a good choice because of the strong relationship between background and the wooden art furniture shown in the inset photos. The textured background also contrasts nicely with the simple, still-life photos of the furniture. The warm coloration of the twigs warms the spread and gives it a rough hewn quality. Dropping the photos into oval shapes rather than rectangular ones gives the spread an elegant quality that balances the roughness of the background texture.

Using Illustrations

Illustrations can communicate your message at a glance. They can emphasize or interpret a headline, establish a particular mood or feeling, and give an emotion or idea tangible form. They can bring out an aspect of your message that isn't readily apparent to the reader or tell a pictorial and written story with good graphic information and a caption. They make your message more memorable because people remember pictures better than words.

Although illustrations are great attention-getters, they are most effective when they reinforce your message. Type and illustrations should be planned so they work together to produce the effect you want. Don't use illustrations as filler or just to "make a piece look better."

When you're considering how to use an illustration and what style or medium it should be in, ask yourself what you want it to achieve. How will it relate to the headline or copy? Will this type of illustration attract your audience? (Remember that "attract" doesn't always mean "appeal to"; it can also mean "startle" or "frighten.") Flip through design magazines such as *HOW* or *Communication Arts* to see what styles have been used in pieces similar to yours. Look at the annual of the Society of Illustrators and creative directories such as *American Showcase: Illustration* for more ideas.

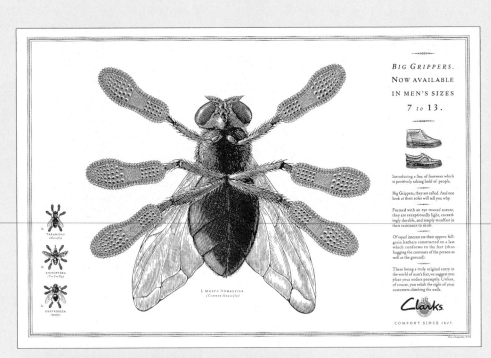

A fly and trees wearing shoes are definitely images that would be impossible to photograph and are extremely difficult to create even with a photo manipulation program. Many effects, such as showing a completely impossible event, can only be created with an illustration. These unusual ideas, translated in a classic woodcut style, makes the reader do a double take. It is classic looking with a visual twist.

This illustration is an interpretation of the doctor's quote positioned on the bottom right. The combination of a realistic photo of the person speaking with an interpretive image of what she is saying is unusual and intriguing. The visuals introduce the idea behind the article, drawing you in so the copy can bring home the message.

An illustration is often the only way to create an effect or the best way to show a subject, including:

- Showing a product or a building that doesn't exist yet.

- Showing a completely impossible event, such as a tree wearing shoes.

- Explaining an abstract idea, such as depression.

- Creating commentary—the special role of editorial illustration, cartoons and caricatures.

- Showing how something was or is put together (medical and technical illustration such as a cutaway view that shows how a muscle or an engine looks and works).

- Showing detail (botanical illustrations give a clear view of one part of a plant).

- Giving a piece an appropriate period look with an illustration in that period's style (delicate images in ornately drawn line art says "Victorian").

Clip Art

Sometimes you need art for a piece and don't have the budget to buy any. What can you do? In many cases clip art may be the answer to your problem. Clip art is ready-to-use illustrations that you can place in your layouts without first getting permission or paying a fee for usage. Today clip art comes both printed and in digital form.

Clip art has an image problem because it is seen as "canned art" and therefore unoriginal; some collections now look dated, also. Customize clip art to give it a fresh look. Combine several pieces to create a new image. Add color or alter the size of part of a piece of clip art. If you're working with a computer graphics program, the possibilities for combining and altering clip art are endless.

Clip art can also work effectively "as is" when handled carefully and in a manner appropriate for a piece. Don't mix styles and periods of clip art in a single piece. Pick one and stick with it to create a specific look or develop a theme. For example, whimsical, Victorian illustrations can create a playful piece.

Never plop clip art down at random to fill empty spots in your layout. Plan its use just as you would any other illustration. Use clip art instead of bullets for lists or to call attention to a headline or a sidebar.

Clip art can be very effective for spot illustrations. Break up a calendar of events for a music festival with a few clip art pictures of musical instruments.

Copyright-free illustrations (clip art) break up the copy in a playful manner. Sprinkling the illustrations throughout the piece attracts the eye to each bit of copy and helps hold the reader's attention. Although the newsletter is copy heavy, the numerous illustrations make the copy easier to get through and more enjoyable. Clip art is an easy, inexpensive way to use a large number of illustrations in a piece.

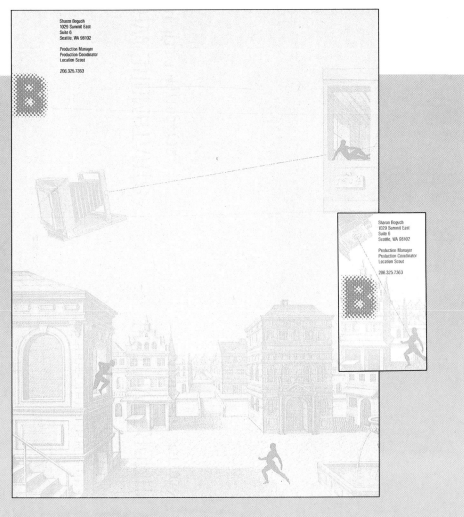

A collage of several pieces of clip art creates fanciful locations. The old camera and the silhouetted figures that appear on each piece subtly describe the client's occupation: location scout, production manager and production coordinator.

This is a partial list of sources to get you started:

Dover Books (print)
31 E. Second St.
Mineola, NY 11501
(516) 294-7000

Graphic Source Clip Art Library (print)
Graphic Products Corporation
1480 S. Wolf Rd.
Wheeling, IL 60090
(708) 537-9300

North Light Books (print)
1507 Dana Ave.
Cincinnati, OH 45207
(513) 531-2222
(800) 289-0963

Clipper (print)/Electronic Clipper (digital)
Subscription only
Dynamic Graphics
6000 N. Forest Park Dr.
P.O. Box 1901
Peoria, IL 61656-9941
(309) 688-8800
(800) 255-8800
fax: (309) 688-5873

Cassady & Greene (digital)
22734 Portola Dr.
Salinas, CA 93908-1119
(408) 484-9218
(800) 359-4920

ClickArt EPS Illustrations (digital)
T/Maker Co.
1390 Villa St.
Mountain View, CA 94041
(415) 962-0195

Image Club (digital)
1902 11th St., S. E., #5
Calgary, Alberta T2G 3G2, CANADA
(403) 262-8008
(800) 661-9410

Getting Art Created

Sometimes you'll need an illustration that you can't create yourself. Then you'll have to hire an illustrator to do it for you. Finding the right illustrator to create the perfect illustration can make a great difference in the success of your piece. It can bring an article to vivid life or make an ad more memorable.

Begin your search for the right illustrator by preparing a design brief for the job. If you have a very clear idea of what the illustration should look like, give a very tight brief to the illustrator who will then create an illustration with the specific image and style you've requested.

When you look for an illustrator, keep in mind how much input you will want as well as the style, medium and kind of illustration needed. As you look at samples of work, note the size of the image and the illustrator's technique. Some people produce only small works and others work on a very large scale. Some people create delicate works with fine lines or tiny details that won't reproduce well small or on coarse papers.

At other times you may want more input from the illustrator. This is especially true of editorial illustrations; these are most often interpretive, conveying a mood or an abstract concept. In these cases, you may set parameters such as size, give some guidelines or suggestions, or state the concept and let the illustrator show you some ideas.

THE DEAD OF WINTER

ILLUSTRATION BY JOHN PATRICK

43 CINCINNATI August 1991

Artist's representatives and individual illustrators send out promotional materials so designers can see samples of an illustrator's work. Samples acquaint you with someone's work if you haven't seen it before or recently. It's easier to decide if someone's style is right for your project when you can see previous work.

Here are some materials showing the work of John Patrick. Because of the richness of his style and content of his work, we selected him for a series of magazine covers, including the one on the facing page.

The final illustration as seen on the cover. This illustration vividly interprets the theme of the issue, "It All Comes Down to People." It encourages employees to explore the contents of the issue and to continue thinking about the key message.

When you work with an illustrator, ask these questions before giving a job:

- What is your background?

- How fast do you work?

- What mediums do you regularly work in?

- What do you feel are your strengths?

- Who are your regular clients?

- Do you have any scheduling conflicts?

- What will you bill for the final illustration? for one-time usage? for a complete buy-out?

- Do you have a fax?

Questions you should ask yourself at the end of a job include:

- How well did I work with that illustrator? Was the illustrator cooperative? Did she have good ideas?

- How did the illustrator respond to requests for alterations and how quickly were they made?

- Was the work delivered on time?

- If the work was late, was that due to circumstances beyond the illustrator's control?

- Were there any aspects of the illustrator's technique such as delicacy of finish that I should remember in the future?

Working With Photographs

The highly graphic or representational nature of photography makes it a potent medium for communication. Photography has great credibility; in fact, people often confuse photos with reality because of their literal and documentary appearance. Pick photos for their capacity to carry meaning, not because they are pretty. Many outstanding public service ads have grotesque or frightening images to drive home their points; they're not pretty images, but they are hard to forget.

Photographs can capture minute details and fleeting human emotions, leading readers to feel they are sharing in that moment. This sense of immediacy and involvement will let you put the reader into the picture, imagining that they are visiting an exotic tourist destination or using an attractive product. The bulk of tourism ads show a scene as if the reader were actually looking at it in order to promote the feeling "I could be there looking at this gorgeous beach and having a great time."

Photos quickly draw readers into your piece. They also promote a feeling of familiarity by showing readers who or what they are reading about. A mug shot (a head shot) of a columnist or VIP creates a more personal relationship with the reader. Even if people don't remember a product's name, they will often remember what it looks like because a photo has made them familiar with its appearance.

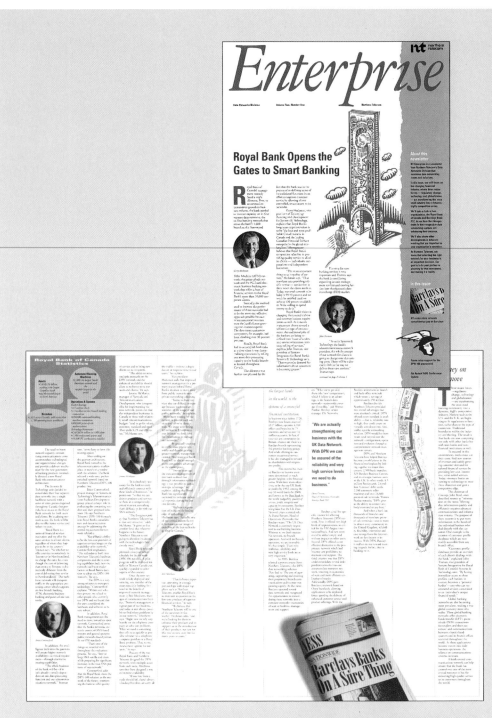

Mug shots don't always have to be squared up. Here they are placed in circles to break up the boxed grid and permit some interesting cropping. Notice that all the faces are approximately the same size and scale, giving each person equal importance.

Who wouldn't want to go to the tropical paradise captured in these vibrant photographs? Four-color photographs in travel brochures help potential travelers imagine themselves in the pictured destinations. Notice that the edges of the big photos have been left soft and unfinished to give these photos the feeling of fine art. The small photos with their jewel-like colors break up the copy, but also lead the reader through it.

Once you have a photo in hand, you have many options for using it in your layout. You can:

• Crop away unneeded or unwanted elements of the photograph to make it better or stronger.

• Crop a photo in an unexpected way, such as putting a mug shot in a star shape to add interest.

• Convert a poor quality color photo to black-and-white; this can often salvage a needed image.

• Bleed it (extend the image beyond one or more edges of a page) to add surprise and impact.

• Outline a photo (strip away the background) to introduce an interesting shape into your layout.

• Outline part of a photo so it breaks out of an otherwise square or rectangular photo (the hood of a speeding car breaks out of its rectangular photo to suggest motion).

• Wrap text around an outlined photograph to break up copy in an exciting visual way.

• Jump the gutter with photos to unify a spread, literally linking the pages together.

• Give readers a sneak preview of a publication by including a small photo from each article with that article's listing in the table of contents.

Getting the Right Photo

There are two primary ways to get the photo or photos you need. You can commission a photographer to create an original image or get one from a stock photo agency. For a fee based on how the image will be used, stock agencies make available large collections of images from many photographers. Whether you commission an image or get it from stock depends on what you need, what your budget is, and when you need the photo.

Product shots always have to be commissioned unless your client already has an appropriate photo. There's little chance that a stock agency will have a shot of McMurdo's Whizbang Widget. Some location shots, such as the client's new factory, and portraits or group shots of special people, must also be commissioned. Other shots can be obtained from stock agencies. They have hundreds of photos of generic locations, such as farms, and of major tourist destinations, such as Paris. Stock agencies also have hundreds of generic shots of people doing a broad range of activities.

When would you use a stock agency instead of getting an original image? To meet budgets and deadlines. Sending a photographer to Hawaii to shoot models frolicking on the beach is expensive. For much less money you can have your pick of dozens of photos of gorgeous people enjoying Hawaiian beaches. Ordering an image from a stock agency can also save you time. Most stock agencies offer overnight delivery, and you can cut up or make color photocopies of your chosen image from the stock catalog to use in a comp.

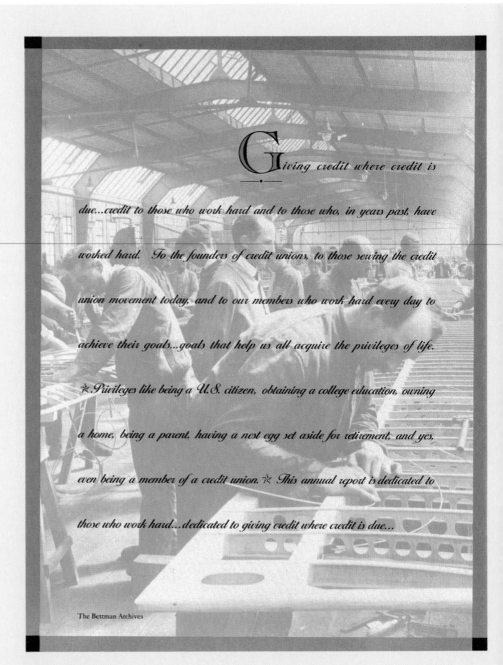

*G*iving credit where credit is due...credit to those who work hard and to those who, in years past, have worked hard. To the founders of credit unions, to those serving the credit union movement today, and to our members who work hard every day to achieve their goals...goals that help us all acquire the privileges of life. ✕ *Privileges like being a U.S. citizen, obtaining a college education, owning a home, being a parent, having a nest egg set aside for retirement, and yes, even being a member of a credit union. ✕ This annual report is dedicated to those who work hard...dedicated to giving credit where credit is due...*

The Bettman Archives

The historical duotone from a stock agency provides an appropriate backdrop for the overlapping introductory copy. It sets the mood for the piece effectively. It would cost too much to recreate and photograph a scene like this. A stock house (some specialize in such historical images) can easily, and often inexpensively, provide such a glimpse of history.

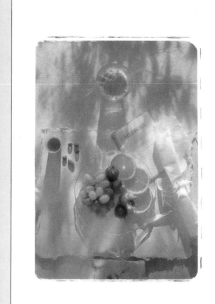

You can almost feel the warmth of the sunshine pouring into this shot. Although it's a simple still life, the angle at which it was photographed and the way it was lit turns it into a unique, memorable image. The warmth of the shot reinforces the copy's message perfectly. Although stock houses carry a wide variety of subjects shot to achieve different effects and moods, it's unlikely any house will have a series of (or sometimes even just one) very specific images with certain effects. In such cases, you'll need to hire a photographer who can create the look you want; the two of you will plan the shots and obtain the props or whatever else is needed to create what you have in mind.

You can locate commercial photographers through recommendations from fellow designers or printers or you can use national directories to locate photographers who have the style or the specialization you need. The major showcases are:

American Showcase
724 Fifth Ave.
New York, NY 10019

New York Gold
724 Fifth Ave.
New York, NY 10019

The Silver Book
American Society of Media Photographers (ASMP)
419 Park Ave. S., Ste. 1407
New York, NY 10016

You can often obtain inexpensive stock images from museums, historical societies, university archives and government agencies.

Although they will be more expensive than the local stock sources, stock photo agencies have a wide selection of images. You can find lists of stock photo agencies, picture libraries and archives in:

ASMP Stock Photography Handbook, 2nd ed.
American Society of Media Photographers
419 Park Ave. S., Ste. 1407
New York, NY 10016

Photographer's Dispatch
AG Editions
142 Bank St., #GA
New York, NY 10014

Photographer's Market
Writer's Digest Books
1507 Dana Ave.
Cincinnati, OH 45207

Illustration or Photograph?

It's often hard to decide whether your layout calls for illustrations or photographs or a combination of both. While there aren't any rules for what will work best, consider what you want the visual to achieve. Illustrations can create effects that can't be achieved easily with photography. Black-and-white photos have a journalistic quality while color photographs create an idealized reality.

Illustrations are often perceived as being less literal and more imaginative than photographs. So, illustration is often more effective than photography for editorial comment, fiction or interpretation. Illustration is a valuable tool for showing abstract concepts or depicting something that doesn't exist yet.

Black-and-white photos convey a feeling of gritty realism and immediacy. They also convey a feeling of spontaneity, a slice-of-life quality like snapshots. Black-and-white photographs have an obvious advantage over full-color ones when it comes to printing costs. They break up a gray, text-heavy page without the expense of four-color printing.

Sometimes you must have a color photo. You may have an image that would simply not work in black and white—a bridge in golden morning light, for example. Food doesn't look very appetizing in black and white either. Sometimes color is a critical part of the subject; readers need to see that paradise has bright blue water and green palm trees (especially when it's winter where they are).

Black-and-white photography gives readers the sense that they are there—a part of an event. Although these photos convey a feeling of reportage (suggested by the tie to the black-and-white news photos we see in the paper each day), they also have a casual, slice-of-life, snapshot feeling. Black-and-white photos can add interest to your layouts by suggesting either an intimate, family feeling or a crisp, factual look. A good black-and-white photo with a range of values will give your piece a rich look at a lower cost than four-color images.

Creative four-color photography can make objects that are usually ordinary—even ugly—more interesting and attractive. The vibrant red communicates a feeling of heat almost like molten lava and makes the whole spread look exciting. We are intrigued by the color and the odd-looking object even if we have no idea what it is. A black-and-white photo of the same object would not be as effective.

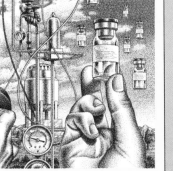

The combination of photographic portraits with elaborate pen-and-ink artwork demonstrates the different strengths of illustration and photography. The photographs give a realistic image of each person. But since these people are talking about very abstract and complex topics, the illustration below them provides a running interpretation of what each is saying far better than a photo could. Objects that would be difficult to combine or juxtapose in a photograph easily mix and mingle in an imaginary landscape.

Choosing & Fixing Photos

The ideal photograph will reproduce well *and* convey just the right mood for the piece. When you have the time and budget, you can often get that ideal image. At other times, you must choose the best photo from the batch.

Determining the reproduction quality of a photo is a straightforward job. A photo is overexposed, underexposed or properly exposed; it is in focus or it isn't. If you can't tell what the subject is, you won't use that photo. (You can sometimes salvage a photo by cropping, reducing its size, or employing some production tricks, but use such measures only as a last resort.)

Choosing the photo that best captures the mood or feeling of your piece can be more difficult. Glance quickly over the sheet, then look away. Did one photo jump out at you? That will be the one with the most impact. Think about the mood you want to create and study the lighting in each. A photo with warm, bright lighting won't create a sad or mysterious mood. When looking at mug shots, consider which photos make the subject look most attractive and which ones best capture the subject's personality. Also consider the direction the subject is looking because the reader's eye will often move in the same direction. Place a photo looking to the right if you want to lead the reader off the cover and into the newsletter. Avoid placing a photo of someone looking left in the left margin; it will lead readers out of your piece.

Contact sheets let you see and evaluate each frame of film before you make a print of any image. To select the best frame, look for definite tone values between adjacent grays, sharp focus, and tonal quality in areas of interest, such as faces. Facial expression is also very important in a portrait. Watch out for blur or motion on people shots. People move, and that movement can sometimes show up as soft focus.

rement Community is
00 Compton Road in
g area of north-
County.

f the Francis-
h System of
i, Inc., St.
dent
urnished
and
ing beds.
d services
gned to
to
ndepen-
a safe and
ere.

971, St. Clare
rly known as
Terrace. Designed
zation in mind, the build-
in four hexagon-shaped units
esidents to visit with their

attention an
Sisters who s
St. Clare Guil
in making St. C
for its residents t
volunteer efforts. A
operates the gift shop, i
stocks items ranging from t
cards to small gifts.

It's frustrating to receive bad quality photos from a client that you must use. But there are ways to make a bad photo look acceptable. As shown on this page, you can drop a photo into a shape or outline it, deleting unnecessary background. You can also surround an outlined image with a solid color or a texture or make it into a duotone.

If you have to use a poor quality photo, here are a few tricks to use to salvage that photo:

• Crop out the background and outline a person's head to get rid of a inconsistent, busy background.

• Drop a photo into a visual shape such as a star or a circle, cropping out unnecessary parts of the photo.

• Run an out of focus photo as a grainy mezzotint to make the soft quality seem intentional and give the photo an illustrative quality.

• Drop in a new, illustrated background around an outlined image.

• Translate the photo into a line or texture screen (most typesetters can do this conversion for you).

• Convert a color photo with poor contrast to black and white, but make sure to have a black-and-white internegative made from the color transparency before you convert it.

• Print on a coated or smooth stock for best reproduction of detail. (If you work with a client who consistently gives you poor quality photos, specify a better stock from the beginning.)

• If lack of contrast is the only problem with a black-and-white photo, consider running it as a duotone to enhance the contrast and give it a rich coloration.

• Have the photo retouched to remove unnecessary details or unwanted parts.

E M P L O Y E E S P O T L I G H T

Editor's Note: All "Spotlight" employees were recommended by their coworkers, who wrote the descriptions on this and the next page.

Thanks to those of you who submitted entries. "Employee Spotlight" is an ongoing feature, if your entry is not included in this issue, it may be in an upcoming

Nineteen Dallas District employees, Southwest Division, Dallas

Front row (left to right) Mary Ellen Payton, Deborah Davis, Claudia Garza, Elizabeth Pelzl, Sherry Wolbrink, Jim Moffett. Back Row (left to right) Don Carpenter, Sandy Justman, April

Cropping & Scaling

Sometimes artwork has elements that you don't want to reproduce. A photograph has an ugly building in the background that you don't want to show or you need to show only one person out of group. In these cases, you'll need to crop (eliminate) those unwanted areas.

Cropping is not done by physically trimming the art. Instead you will place crop marks on the artwork to show the selected areas. If you place the crop marks in the margins of the image, use short lines placed at right angles to each other to mark the corners of the selected area. You can also mark the crop on a tissue or tracing paper overlay taped to the artwork. With this method you can draw a box around the area selected for reproduction.

You also need to scale art—resize it—to fit your layout. Artwork can be enlarged or reduced depending on the size of the original and how it will fit in the layout. However, images keep the same proportions when enlarged or reduced. A thin, vertical photo will not get wider as it gets shorter.

To accurately scale art, you must carefully measure the exact dimensions it will have in the printed piece. Compare that measurement with the actual dimensions of your piece of art. If it is larger than the opening, it must be reduced; if it is smaller than the opening, it must be enlarged. For example, if your photo is a four-inch square and it must fit into a three-inch square space, it will be reproduced at 75 percent of its original size. If your photo is four-inches square and must fit into a six-inch square space, it will be reproduced at 150 percent of its original size.

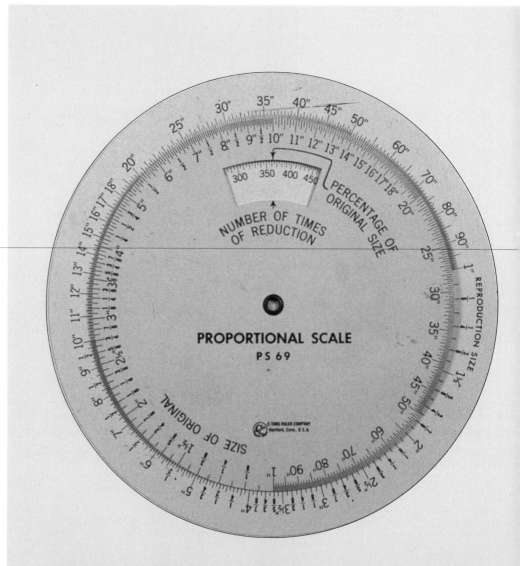

When you use a proportion wheel to determine the percentage of enlargement or reduction you'll need, you align the size you have (on the inner wheel) with the size you want (the outer wheel) and look up your percentage on the scale in the window. A proportion wheel is a good tool for learning how to scale art, but it is less accurate than doing it with a calculator. As soon as you feel confident scaling with the wheel, try to work out percentages with a calculator (divide what you want by what you have and then multiply by 100 if you're not using a calculator with a percent function) and check the results against the wheel.

Notice in the full-frame shot that there is a lot of extraneous detail surrounding the focus—the people. This detail will detract from what the viewer should pay attention to in the piece. Crop marks have been placed outside the picture area in grease pencil. These marks tell the printer how to frame the photo.

You can use either a proportion wheel or a calculator to determine percentages of enlargement or reduction. A proportion wheel shows the size of the original on the inner wheel, the reproduction size on the outer wheel, and the percentage of original size in a window on the dial. To use a proportion wheel:

1. Determine the dimensions the will have in the printed piece.

2. Measure the art.

3. Align either dimension (depth or width) of the actual art on the inner wheel with the reproduction size on the outer wheel.

4. Write down the percentage that appears in the window.

To use a calculator:

1. Determine the dimensions the art will have in the printed piece.

2. Measure the art.

3. Using either dimension (depth or width) divide the final size of the actual printed piece by the actual size of the art. In other words, divide what you want by what you have.

4. Write down the result—converting the decimal to a percentage (0.4 equals 40 percent), carrying the result out to one-tenth of a percent (0.415 equals 41.5 percent).

Cropping in tightly to the people leaves only a dark, consistent background. The image has been enlarged from the original, so it will fit into the space planned for it in the layout. A tag should be attached to each piece of art, labeled so the art can be matched to the mechanical, and marked with the percentage of enlargement or reduction. This image is 50 percent (one-and-one-half times) the size of the original, so the tag would have been marked for reproduction at 150 percent.

Special Effects

A photograph can be more than a representation of reality. When used with flair and good judgment, special effects applied to photographs can create dramatic results. By using special line screens, a photograph can be made to look like fine art—an engraving, a mezzotint or a painting. You can add a splash of color for little extra cost with a duotone or a flat tint halftone. With a photo manipulation computer program, a photo can be distorted, rearranged and otherwise altered to give your layout a totally unique look. (If you don't have such a program, many service bureaus will produce manipulated images for you.)

Plan your use of special effects images; they're no substitute for a good concept or a well-executed layout. Think about what you want to achieve with an image. For example, get a black-and-white photo of a historical site and have a duotone printed in warm brown and black to create the illusion of a vintage photo.

You'll get the best results if you begin with a good quality photograph. Although slight defects in a photo can sometimes be covered up (you can make a photo that's soft into a mezzotint, for example), it's best not to gamble. There are many paper promotions that show the results of different kinds of line screens, duotones and other special effects techniques and explain how to produce them. Consult your printer about the capabilities of the press your piece will be printed on. Printers generally will have samples that show special effects achieved for other clients.

This poster shows many different uses for the computer manipulation of images. They're placed inside skewed shapes or on top of each other, made transparent, cropped, outlined and distorted. The photos interact and become an intriguing collage that the viewer can study, discovering new things over time.

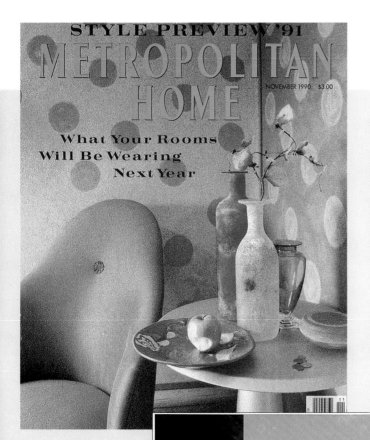

You can actually see the individual dots of color that create this mezzotint. The image appears to be a painting rather than a photo because of the texture. The mezzotint screen gives the image a grainy quality that makes it look and feel very different from a traditional four-color image. Keep in mind that not every subject will work as a mezzotint. If your subject matter warrants a dreamlike, romantic look, a mezzotint might be the answer.

Screening back a four-color image can create a beautiful textural backdrop for typography as seen here. The value contrasts among the strong, black band, the full strength orange photo inside the letterform, and the soft background add to the beauty of the piece. Ghosted four-color imagery is perfect for times when you want an interesting background for overprinting type, a hint of an image, or a contrast between strong and soft.

Here are some of the most frequently used special photographic effects:

• Duotone: a two-color halftone made from a regular black-and-white photograph that has been shot once for the black plate and once for the color plate.

• Double-black duotone: a duotone that has been printed with two black plates to match the rich solid blacks of a glossy photograph.

• Flat-tint halftone: a black-and-white halftone is surprinted over a flat background tint of a second color.

• Tritone: a black-and-white photo reproduced using three ink colors.

• Ghosted halftone: the image is much lighter than a normal halftone.

• Posterization: a high-contrast line shot made from continuous tone copy.

• Line conversion: conversion of continuous tone copy to a line shot with special line screens that produce special effects including wavy, vertical straight and circular line patterns.

• Mezzotint : a line conversion that gives a soft hand-drawn or handpainted look.

• Vignette: a halftone in which the edges fade until only the paper is visible, producing a soft edge.

• Manipulation: the alteration of a halftone, usually done on a computer, to create a wide range of special effects, including posterization, distortion, blurring, embossing, diffusing, faceting and digitizing (giving an image a pixellated appearance).

More Effects & Retouching

Retouching a photograph—altering it by removing unwanted background or strengthening detail—is similar to creating special effects images because special tools are used to make a new image out of an original photograph. Although retouching generally involves eliminating flaws, it can also be used to make bold changes. Eyes can be changed from blue to green or portions of two or more photos can be combined into a single image.

Retouching tools and techniques have changed dramatically; retouching by hand or with an airbrush has been replaced by electronic retouching. (The fast pace of change will continue as making color separations and making color corrections on the desktop becomes more common.) Images can be scanned into a desktop computer or a dedicated prepress system for color corrections (changes made to color, contrast or tone), image improvements (eliminating a facial blemish or erasing part of a background) or substantial alterations. If you have enough time, airbrushing or hand retouching can cost less than scanning in a photo and paying for the time of the operator who works on it, but conventional retouching can take up to a week, and then you'll still need to get the separations made.

Retouching can get you out of a jam by fixing an important photo so it can be used. But a retouched photo never looks as good as one that was right to begin with. When a color cast or underexposure is corrected, for example, contrast will be gained at the expense of some shadow and highlight detail. Retouching should, therefore, be a last resort rather than a habit.

Duotones (two color halftones made from black-and-white photos) can be printed in many different color combinations. The top duotone is printed with cyan and black, the bottom one with magenta and black. Duotones give you a richer looking image than black-and-white halftones. Just be sure to pick the right color for the mood of your piece. Many paper companies have produced demonstration pieces on duotones. Contact a local merchant if you need more information.

The screened back black-and-white image that continues the square-finish (rectangular, straight-edged) four-color image creates an interesting contrast in value and shape. The black-and-white imagery seems to blend right into the page in parts—activating the image and giving the page movement.

Sometimes you will need to remove unwanted elements from a photograph rather than spend time and money to shoot another one. We needed a shot of the oldest tree in the community. Unfortunately, it was in a cemetery surrounded by headstones! An airbrush illustrator was able to retouch the photo and remove the headstones. This left the desired image of tree and grass as you see in the detail of the photo shown here.

A Few Last Words

In this chapter we've shown you many ways to use visuals and graphics to beautify and communicate. In order to maximize your use of these elements in your layout, there are a few points about how color printing works that you will need to keep in mind when making a layout.

Flat (solid) colors are printed with a single ink. These colors should be chosen from a color matching system that gives a swatchbook of ink samples to use in communicating with your printer. You can use flat colors to create duotones (tritones, quadtones, etc.), screen tints behind type, rules and colored type, among other uses.

Four-color process printing is used to reproduce full-color images. You can also produce screen tints, colored rules, etc., in a variety of colors along with your full-color image. When printed, the four process colors appear as dots of color combined in various sizes and patterns that reproduce the full range of colors found in the original image. The dot patterns are produced from color separations, one separation (a piece of screened film used to make a printing plate) is produced for each of the four colors. Specify the line screen (a finely cross-ruled plate that breaks up continuous-tone images, such as illustrations, into dot patterns) you want for the color separations. A 133-line screen is slightly coarse, a 150-line screen gives a good, standard reproduction, while a 175-line screen produces an extremely crisp image.

If you are creating custom colors for rules, tint screens or other graphic elements on your desktop computer, remember that what you see may not be what you get. Even if you are using a color matching system, the difference between the way your monitor produces color and the way the printing press produces color can alter the appearance of a color. Check your choices against printed swatches on the right kind of stock (coated paper yields different results than uncoated paper).

Use a color matching system if you are coordinating the colors to be printed on a letterhead system with corporate colors. This enables you to make sure that everyone involved with the job understands just what color you have in mind. It also helps with quality control later. If someone else will reprint a letterhead you produced, they may define "warm red" differently than you do. It's harder to misunderstand "Red #665."

Flat colors come in colors that are not easily reproduced in process colors. Lemon yellows, reddish purples, bright greens and some oranges are very difficult to achieve; metallics cannot be created at all. If you have a visual that features one of these colors or want to use such a color as a graphic element, investigate the costs of printing a fifth color in addition to the four process colors to get the result you want.

Chapter 3
Putting It All Together

New non-rub ink
covers the news,
not you.

San Francisco Examiner
The Afternoon Paper

Type and visuals are the building blocks of any layout. It's how you put them together that makes the difference between a good layout and one that isn't. Making a good layout involves bringing order to the type and visuals needed to communicate your message. If people can't easily find their way through a piece and understand it, they won't try for very long. That means a good layout directs and redirects visual traffic so readers arrive at the right destination.

A good layout begins with a carefully thought out concept. Then all the materials needed to communicate that concept are shaped, refined and rearranged until they clearly present the desired message. Every layout must take account of its format, audience, environment and intent. Who will see it? What should it say? Where will it be seen?

Last, but far from least, good layouts must attract. How important is this? Very. Good layouts attract and hold readers, while bad layouts drive them away. If shoppers don't like what they see in the window, they won't come in and buy.

This chapter shows how to combine the building blocks—type and visuals—into good layouts.

Formats: Newsletters

The first step in working on a newsletter is to determine its format: the size and number of pages. Sometimes the format will be driven by how the newsletter will be used. A newsletter that's to be kept for reference would be 8½"x11" and three-hole punched for storage in a binder. A tabloid-size format (11"x17") will make the piece stand out in the mail.

The amount of copy you have also determines the size and the number of pages you'll need. A tabloid-size newsletter gives you more room for copy and larger visuals. If you won't have much copy, an be 8½"x11" and three-hole punched format is a better choice. If you don't know how much copy each issue will have, slant your format toward having too much rather than too little material.

Nonstandard formats, such as 9"x12", can be effective, especially if competitors use newsletters, too. Before finalizing the layout, ask the postal service what the mailing cost will be and discuss any extra costs with your client. Mailing weight can also affect the number of pages you'll have; often the material for an issue will be cut to save mailing costs. If your newsletter will be saddle stitched (bound by stapling the sheets where they fold at the spine), your number of pages must be a multiple of four.

Most newsletters are mailed folded, because they're less expensive to mail that way. Many are self-mailers to avoid the cost of envelopes. If yours is self-mailing, be sure to leave enough room at the bottom of the back page for a label and other mailing information.

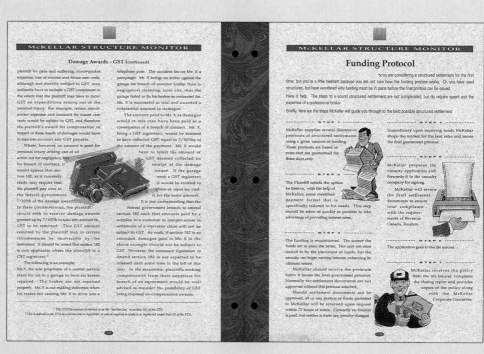

This newsletter was designed so the recipient could keep all of the issues together in a binder. The 8½"x11", hole-punched, four-page newsletter is compact and clean. The similar graphic format of each issue holds them together as a set.

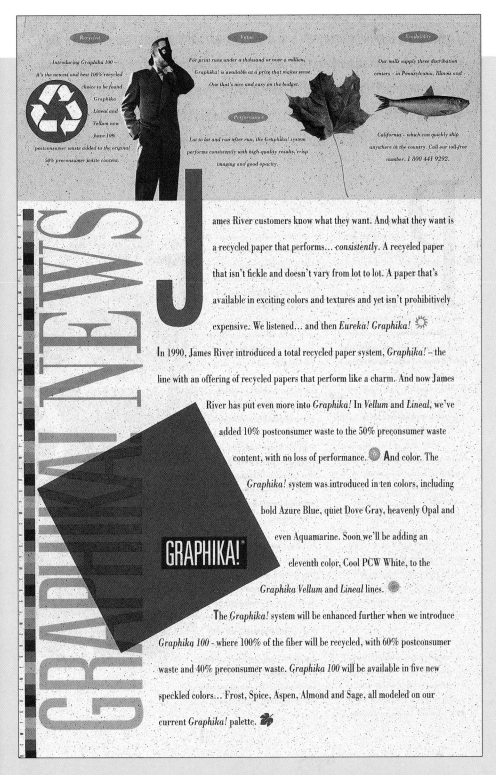

GRAPHIKA NEWS

James River customers know what they want. And what they want is

a recycled paper that performs... *consistently*. A recycled paper

that isn't fickle and doesn't vary from lot to lot. A paper that's

available in exciting colors and textures and yet isn't prohibitively

expensive. We listened... and then *Eureka! Graphika!*

In 1990, James River introduced a total recycled paper system, *Graphika!* – the

line with an offering of recycled papers that perform like a charm. And now James

River has put even more into *Graphika!* In *Vellum* and *Lineal,* we've

added 10% postconsumer waste to the 50% preconsumer waste

content, with no loss of performance. **A**nd color. The

Graphika! system was introduced in ten colors, including

bold Azure Blue, quiet Dove Gray, heavenly Opal and

even Aquamarine. Soon we'll be adding an

GRAPHIKA!®

eleventh color, Cool PCW White, to the

Graphika Vellum and *Lineal* lines.

The *Graphika!* system will be enhanced further when we introduce

Graphika 100 – where 100% of the fiber will be recycled, with 60% postconsumer

waste and 40% preconsumer waste. *Graphika 100* will be available in five new

speckled colors... Frost, Spice, Aspen, Almond and Sage, all modeled on our

current *Graphika!* palette.

The tabloid-size newsletter gave the designer a lot of flexibility in creating a layout. He was able to use large type and more visuals than would have been possible with an 8¹/₂"x11" newsletter. Offbeat visuals and the oversized, colorful letterforms of the title and drop cap create an exciting, inviting piece.

When you're selecting a format for a newsletter, here are some considerations to keep in mind:

• Amount of copy and number of visuals per issue. If there won't be a lot of copy or many visuals that can be run large, 8¹/₂"x11" is your best choice. Lots of copy and visuals will substantially increase the number of 8¹/₂"x11" pages. Tabloid format (11"x17") reduces the number of pages, and thereby the mailing weight.

• How frequently it's published. A weekly newsletter will generally have brief, timely copy that's well suited to the 8¹/₂"x11" format. Quarterly newsletters tend to have a lot of copy and visuals and are, therefore, better suited to the tabloid format.

• Whether it will be filed for future reference. If readers will keep the issues for reference, select an 8¹/₂"x11" format that is hole-punched for use in a three-ring binder.

• Whether it's an informal, chatty publication or more editorial in nature. A company newsletter will generally only run a few pages. A marketing oriented newsletter with strong editorial content may run between twenty-four and thirty-two 8¹/₂"x11" pages and have a separate cover in a format similar to that of a magazine.

• If it needs to stand out in the mail, tabloid-size newsletters and newsletters with a format similar to a magazine command more attention.

• What kind of image it should project. A tabloid-size newsletter can project a newspaper like image, while an 8¹/₂"x11" format can project the image of a press release or a bulletin.

Formats: Brochures

Choosing a brochure format involves more than just deciding how much space you'll need for the copy and pictures. Think first about how it will be used. If a brochure will be mailed, it often must fit into a #10 envelope to avoid the costs of special envelopes and extra postage.

You must also consider the sequence of information as well as breaks in content. When readers must see one panel after another in a tight, predetermined sequence, an accordion fold (the paper is folded in parallel several times, resembling an accordion) works best. With a roll fold (each fold wraps around the previous one) panels are hidden, and readers may accidentally read a panel out of sequence. A gatefold (two panels fold back to reveal a larger, single panel) lets you open up the brochure to a panel where you can show a large visual or block of copy. Whatever format you choose, make sure there are comfortable breaks in the material and that all copy and visuals are placed on the right panels.

Get a paper dummy made by a local paper merchant. This will show you how the brochure looks and feels, and let you check its mailing weight. If you're having the piece bound, show it to your printer. Saddle stitching is inexpensive, but your brochure may have enough pages or weight to require perfect binding (binding edges are roughened by grinding, then an adhesive is applied and the cover attached to the glued edges).

This accordion-folded, multi-panel brochure reveals a lot of imagery when opened, yet it folds into a compact, easy to hold piece. It could almost be used as a mini-poster when fully opened, encouraging the recipient not only to keep the brochure but to display it.

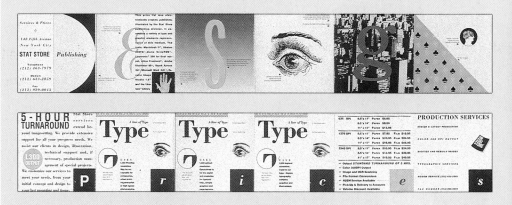

A multi-panel brochure doesn't have to open to a single, sweeping image. Above a different image is presented on each panel while spelling out the single word, "Design", across all of them. The piece as a whole presents an animated collage to the viewer.

Brochures have an almost endless variety of formats. Here are the most commonly used:

- Four-page
- Six-page roll fold
- Six-page accordion fold
- Eight-page roll fold
- Eight-page accordion fold
- Eight-page map fold
- Eight-page gatefold
- Eight-page parallel fold
- Twelve-page broadside
- Sixteen-page broadside
- Sixteen-page booklet, saddle-stitched
- Twenty-four-page booklet, saddle-stitched
- Thirty-two-page booklet, perfect bound

Using the same graphic device, typefaces and type styles (these were inspired by design styles at the time of De Stijl) throughout a multipage brochure makes it easier to read. Placing a box in the upper left corner and the blocky type chosen for the headlines set the look for the whole piece. Once you've chosen the elements that will be consistent, you can freely arrange and vary the rest of the layout on individual spreads.

Formats: Ads

Ad formats are set by the publications in which they appear. Newspaper ads are sold by the column inch; your ad will generally be between two and three columns wide (classifieds are one column wide) and several inches high. The newspaper's sales department can supply you with sizes and rates. Magazines have media kits that include rate cards with sizes and costs.

Large ads attract by their size and allow more room for type, visuals, white space and borders, so go with a large ad whenever possible. Small ads must fight harder for attention with all the other material on the page.

For maximum impact in a small ad, keep your layout simple. Complex ads jammed with words and pictures are much harder to read than those with one or two strong focal points. When planning your layout, provide ample white space so your ad will have enough contrast to stand out.

No matter what size ad you're working on, make sure the copy and visuals are proportioned attractively in the available space. If your ad's shape is strongly horizontal, make your visual a strong horizontal accompanied by small chunks of copy. When working on a tall, thin ad, use a tall, thin visual and group most of your copy at the bottom. Sometimes designing against the shape of your ad can be very effective. Try a series of vertically oriented visuals across a horizontal ad or working with strong diagonals in a tall, thin ad.

A full-page newspaper ad can pack in a lot of information while still being well-organized and eye-catching. Various types of rules, borders and visuals are used to break the ad up into manageable bites. Note how the telephone visual makes the call to action pop out.

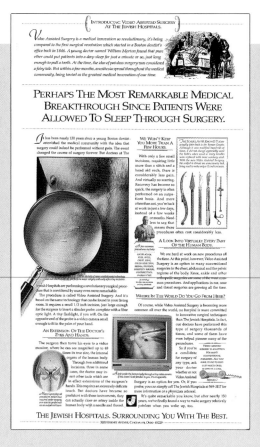

This half-page newspaper ad takes full advantage of the available space by using attention-getting typography and visuals. The silhouetted photos overlap the type to communicate in a novel, subtle way that this is a fashion-related ad. This ad capitalizes on its strong horizontal orientation with horizontal blocks of type and the band of reversed type with its wavy edge. This strong horizontal thrust is countered by the two vertical figures. Their intersection with the type adds even more drama.

The life-size shoe creates the illusion that a real shoe has been dropped on the page you're reading. The copy, which tells the story of the woman who wears this shoe, tightly wraps around the image. Parts of a few words have been omitted to heighten the illusion that the shoe is literally on top of the copy. The bright color of the product logo makes it stand out in the corner and is nicely balanced with the inset photo of the shoe's owner.

Newspaper ads don't come in standard sizes because they're sold in column inches, although half-page and full-page ads are fairly common. Magazine ads do have standard formats, but the actual dimensions of the ad will be determined by the size of the magazine's page, gutter and margins. Check the actual dimensions with the magazine. Standard formats for magazine ads include:

- A spread, non-bleed
- A spread with bleed
- A page, non-bleed
- A page with bleed
- $2/3$ page
- $1/2$-page vertical
- $1/2$-page horizontal
- $1/3$-page square
- $1/3$-page vertical
- $1/4$ page
- $1/6$ page

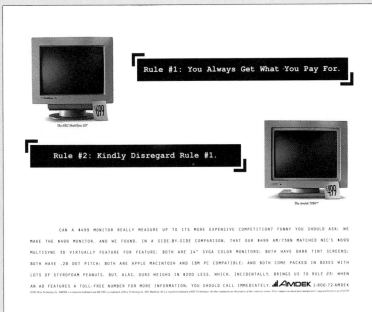

This ad takes full advantage of its horizontal format. The designer set the two-part headline in strong, horizontal black bands surrounded by lots of white space to make sure the whole headline is read first. The friendly, informal tone of the headline copy is reflected in the typewriter type in which it is set. The conversational body copy is given the same informal, friendly feeling with its open letter and line spacing. With the right message and the right amount of white space, a half-page ad could stand out more than a copy heavy full-page ad.

Grids

Making a layout is like putting together a jigsaw puzzle, only you have words, pictures and graphic elements to work with. When you work a jigsaw puzzle, it's usually easiest to put the border together first, and then use it as a framework to decide how the other pieces go together. Grids give you a framework for putting your layouts together. Grids establish the overall structure of a layout by dividing the available space into equally sized columns, margins and spaces. Grids also ensure that you maintain page-to-page and project-to-project consistency. Every ad for a company should have the logo handled the same way in the same place. Newsletters and brochures are easier to read if every page has the same basic structure. But giving every page the same structure does not mean they all look alike.

Make your grid flexible enough to give your pieces variety. With a four-column grid, you could give some pages a single column of type two columns wide and a large visual, while the others have four columns of type mixed with visuals. It's even all right to break your grid occasionally. Bleed photographs or let them jump the gutter, but don't break the grid just to make the page look different or to make your material fit. Those random-looking layouts produced by top designers are the result of much work and skill. Learn to work well within the grid first, and then experiment with it.

Grids give structure, but you have great flexibility when using them. Even though this is clearly a three-column grid, notice that the designer did not completely fill the columns with copy. Visual imagery and large interesting headlines cross over the gridlines, while the body is contained within by large dotted lines. Most of the inside column on the right-hand page of this spread is occupied by a lengthy subhead set in an ornate script face with loose leading. Notice how that inside column has been "split in half" at the top to accommodate the lengthy headline with its huge final word. The first part of the headline, "The Age of Limitless Choice: an Interview with Neville" is stacked to fit into the left half of the column while the *B* of "Brody" gets the other half. The rest of Brody's last name runs across the other two columns on the page.

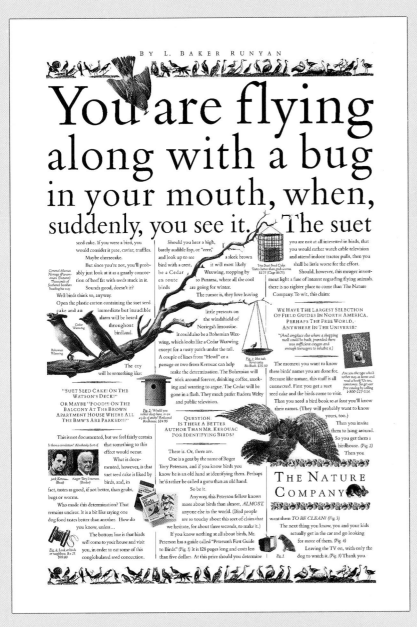

Grids help to organize information but they shouldn't create rigid barriers. This designer used a three-column grid as a base, but then crossed over it in many places with visuals to create a storybook quality for the ad. Notice how the rule between columns one and two becomes the wire of a birdhouse and how a series of bird illustrations becomes the border at the top and bottom of the ad. The key to interrupting type with a visual is to make sure that you break the type in such a way that it is still easily readable. Pay close attention to line breaks in a text wrap; the breaks should fall close to the visual and not interrupt the text in such a way that it might be misunderstood. Note how well copy is broken in column one where the branch falls between sentences.

The most commonly used page size is 8¹/₂"x11". Here are suggestions for ways to divide that page attractively and efficiently:

• Divide it into two columns each 22¹/₂ picas wide with 3 pica side margins (these would be the left and right margins if you're working on a single page, the inside and outside margins if you're working on facing pages) and 1¹/₂ picas between columns (most page layout programs call this spacing the "gutter").

• Divide it into two columns—one 34 picas, the other 9 picas with 3 pica side margins, and reserve 2 picas between columns.

• Divide it into three evenly sized columns, each 14 picas wide with 3 pica side margins and 1¹/₂ picas between columns.

• Divide it into three columns, with the left column 9 picas and the center and right columns 16 picas each, with 3 pica side margins and 2 picas between columns. Use the smaller column for captions, pull quotes, pictures or subheads.

• Divide it into four columns at 10 picas each with 2¹/₂ pica side margins and 2 picas between columns. This format allows for a lot of flexibility when sizing pictures.

• Divide it into four columns, with three columns 11 picas and the left column 8¹/₂ picas, and 2¹/₂ pica side margins and 1¹/₂ picas between columns. Use the smaller column for captions, pull quotes, pictures or subheads.

Grids

The copy is set into a four-column grid, but the central visual interrupts the columns; the copy is forced to run around it. The columns give the ad structure. Breaking the grid calls attention to the visual, loosens the ad up a bit, and makes it more flowing and less geometric. The script letterforms used to begin each paragraph add elegance to the organic flow of the ad, as does the flowing fabric used as a surrounding border texture.

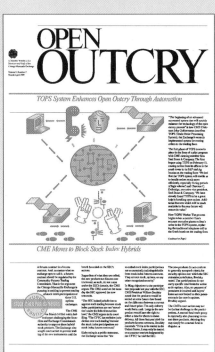

This four-column grid is offset to the right, leaving a large, open margin. The white space gives nice visual relief from the heavy copy or it can be used for small illustrations and captions to add interest. The four-column grid gives designers lots of options for sizing pictures. Here the designer was able to use three-, two- and one-column pictures, in both vertical and horizontal format.

Because the two columns of type are justified and compact, the white callout space cut out of the center creates an interesting value contrast against the gray value of the type. This gives the design a geometric quality that complements that of the illustration. The two-columns also create a very symmetrical, balanced and solid look.

The two columns of this grid are clearly separated by the heavy center rule. The justified columns of type give the page a boxy look that relates well to the boxy, geometric illustration. A two-column grid like this is a good way to make forty pounds of text easily read and attractive to look at, even when the type has to be tiny to fit it all in.

Words Alone Work

Sometimes words are all you need. When there is a strong, verbal message—powerful words that will grab readers—you don't need visuals. Choose a type treatment that showcases that message and let the words work for you. Give a short, sweet headline a big, bold treatment. Dress up long pieces with eye-catching, attractively designed pull quotes.

Always remember that type has a strong visual component. Make every kind of type on the page distinctive but still part of a unified system. Pull a publication together by coming up with a system where every element, even the page numbers, are unified by an aspect of the type treatment. A classic technique for creating this unity is to use one or two weights and styles of a single typeface.

Sometimes words are all you have to work with. Make the most of what you have. Embellish sidebars with contrasting type treatments or tease readers into the copy with enticing subheads. Set the copy in a shape as has been done in the ad on this page. Transform letterforms into objects or decorate letterforms or complete words.

Whatever you do, make sure it's appropriate. If your audience is very visually literate or enjoys exploring complex layers of information, go all out with your type treatments. However, this technique works only on an audience willing and able to invest the time needed to decode your message. Remember that most readers will take only a few seconds to decide if they want to bother with any message.

It's in here. And it's no smaller than a tumor that's found in a real breast. The difference is, while searching for it in this ad could almost be considered fun and games, discovering the real thing could be a matter of life and death. Breast cancer is one of the most common forms of cancer to strike women. And, if detected at an early enough stage, it's also one of the most curable. That's why the American Cancer Society recommends that women over forty have a mammogram at least every other year, and women under forty have a baseline mammogram between the ages of 35 to 39. You see, a mammogram can discover a tumor or a cyst up to three years before you'd ever feel a lump. In fact, it can detect a tumor or a cyst no bigger than a pinhead. Which, incidentally, is about the size of what you are searching for on this page. At Charter Regional in Cleveland, you can have a mammogram performed for just $101. Your mammogram will be conducted in private, and your results will be held in complete confidence and sent directly to your doctor. After your mammogram, a trained radiology technician will meet with you individually and show you how to perform a breast self-examination at home. And, we'll provide you with a free sensor pad, a new exam tool that can amplify the feeling of anything underneath your breast. Something even as small as a grain of salt. If you would like to schedule a mammogram, just call Charter's Call for Health at 593-1210 or 1-800-537-8184. Oh, and by the way, if you haven't found the lump by now, chances are, you're not going to. It was in the 17th line. The period at the end of the sentence was slightly larger than the others. So think about it, if you couldn't find it with your eyes, imagine how hard it would be to find it with your hands.

CAN YOU
FIND
THE LUMP
IN THIS
BREAST?

CHARTER REGIONAL MEDICAL CENTER

CALL FOR HEALTH

5 9 3 . 1 2 1 0

The body copy becomes the visual in this all-type ad. The type is set into an appropriate shape which visually leads the reader into the headline. The ample white space surrounding the breast-shaped copy plays an important role in shaping the body copy. It also accentuates the headline and the hospital's name. This ad would stand out very well in a newspaper full of squared off columns of type.

There's...nuh...thing quite...as...re...ward ing...as...hear....ing an...ad...dult...read for.....the........vair ree......first....time.

The designer didn't need anything more than type to communicate the message in a dramatic way. The type is designed in such a way that the viewer can almost "hear" an adult illiterate sounding out each word. A visual of an adult learning to read would not have the same impact. Making the type somewhat challenging to read promotes the reader's identification with those who struggle to read anything.

You can have an attractive, visually exciting piece even if you have only type to work with. Try these ideas:

- Place the page numbers inside of small shapes that relate to your layout.

- Treat a callout or an initial cap with larger type or a decorative typeface.

- Run body copy in a shape or wrap it around other inset bits of copy.

- Take an existing typeface and modify certain letters or stretch, curve or otherwise alter an entire word to create a masthead or a logotype.

- Simplify a letterform so it becomes a shape that still uniquely communicates the letter, but is also a separate symbol.

- Use hand-drawn or calligraphic lettering to communicate certain emotions, moods or qualities (fluid, elegant calligraphy suggests high quality).

- Contrast a bold sans serif typeface with a quiet serif face to achieve a dramatic effect.

- Use period typefaces to suggest a feeling of the past.

- Contrast a block of copy that has open, airy leading with another chunk that is tightly leaded.

- Intertwine two bits of copy. Weave two paragraphs together by slightly overlapping and running lines of the second paragraph between lines of the first.

- Run a small phrase in the midst of a huge amount of space.

Words Alone Work

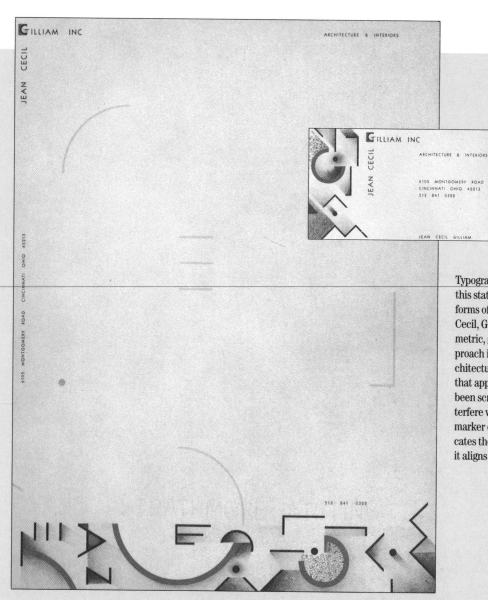

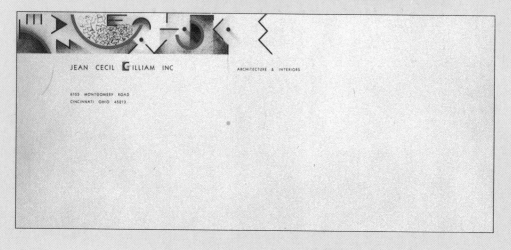

Typography becomes illustration on this stationery system. The letterforms of the client's name, Jean Cecil, Gilliam, Inc., have become geometric, gradated forms. This approach is quite appropriate for an architectural firm. The design elements that appear in the message area have been screened back so they won't interfere with the message. Notice the marker on the envelope that indicates the placement of the address so it aligns with the design.

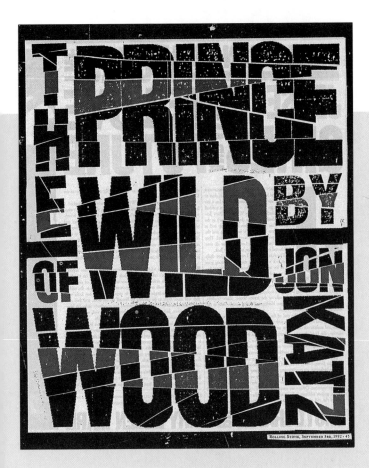

The designer roughened the type on a copying machine, blurring the edges and breaking it up. Then the letters were spliced and moved. This technique is almost painterly. It communicates a feeling of energy and aggression through type alone. The type is the visual.

(Right) This piece is a nice contrast to the "Prince of Wild Wood" piece. Here the hand-drawn, calligraphic letterforms are fluid and very elegant. The movement of the letters perfectly conveys the meaning of the word. The reader can almost hear the music just by looking at this typographic expression.

Pictures Do the Talking

As children, we learn to recognize and to relate to pictures first. As adults we favor pictorial information over the written word because seeing is a simple, effortless action. That means pictures are the fastest way to make your point, especially when a picture needs no explanation.

A self-explanatory picture generally has an easily recognized subject or draws on obvious and well-known symbols. A photo of a sports car speeding down a highway has a definite, familiar connotation. Showing a running cheetah and a sports car makes a point about speed and beauty because the cheetah has long been used as a symbol of these qualities. On the other hand, ostriches are fast moving, but because they are associated with having your head in the sand, showing an ostrich and a sports car won't say "speed" to your audience.

Pictorial logos draw heavily on well-known and easily understood images and visual concepts. A globe says "international"; a camera says "photography." Curved lines and shapes are perceived as friendly, jagged lines as aggressive. Pick the most important aspect of a company and then develop the clearest way to visually communicate it.

Visuals are excellent tools for making the abstract tangible. They let you tug at your reader's emotions. It's one thing to be told why you should give money to a worthy cause; it's another to be faced with a picture of someone who needs help. Being asked to picture yourself in a tropical paradise lacks the immediacy of seeing a tropical paradise and imagining yourself there.

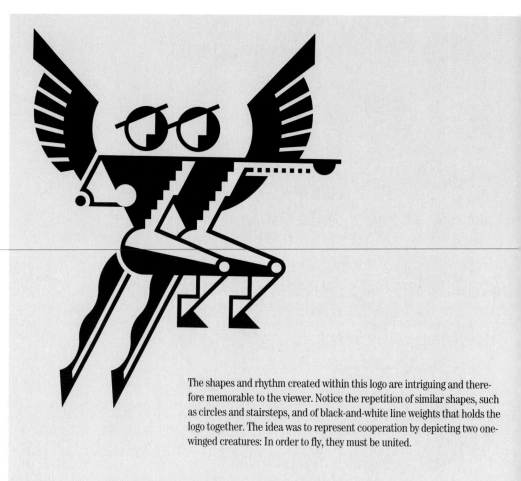

The shapes and rhythm created within this logo are intriguing and therefore memorable to the viewer. Notice the repetition of similar shapes, such as circles and stairsteps, and of black-and-white line weights that holds the logo together. The idea was to represent cooperation by depicting two one-winged creatures: In order to fly, they must be united.

This logo for the Mary Kay Annual Awards Ceremony appropriately uses organic, flowing curves to shape a graphic image of a woman holding flowers. It is even enclosed within a curve. The curves give the symbol a friendly quality. Without any words, this image communicates an impression of a happy woman who is appreciated. No words, but a lot communicated simply.

The striking illustration not only clearly communicates what the product can do for the user but gives the package a dramatic quality. The strong, simple type treatment adds to the dramatic impact. The cover illustration reduces nicely for use on the actual computer disk because the illustration is composed of a few large shapes rather than a lot of little, elaborate ones.

Here are some ideas for ways to use pictures instead of words:

• Replace a word or a letter with a picture that communicates its meaning (a famous poster shows the letter *B* in IBM replaced with a picture of a bee).

• Use a self-explanatory image; sometimes a picture really is worth a thousand words. (An ad for framing shows the results of framing by putting a frame around part of the ad's main visual.)

• Use an illustration or a photo to provoke an emotional response—shock, intrigue, amusement, etc.—without any words at all. (An ad opposing child or animal abuse needs only show the effects of the abuse to produce a reaction.)

• Communicate in shorthand with symbols because they can convey meaning quickly and easily (directional signage or a no smoking sign, for example).

• Deliver an instant message about a company through an illustrated symbol or logo; keep it clear and stylistically appropriate to convey the right message. (A symbol that includes a dog and a cat says "veterinarian.")

• Run a series of sequential pictures side-by-side to communicate a story the same way comic strips do.

• Collage various imagery done for a company to give a quick overview of their industry and expertise. (An image with computers and circuitry shows the company is computer-oriented.)

The images were carefully chosen for this series of book covers to reinforce the textbook subject matter in a unique and thought-provoking manner. Each cover works alone; viewed together they create a powerful system. Always remember that book cover design is packaging design. It's important to understand the market and the distribution methods. Covers often sell the book just the way the box can sell cereal.

Pictures Do the Talking

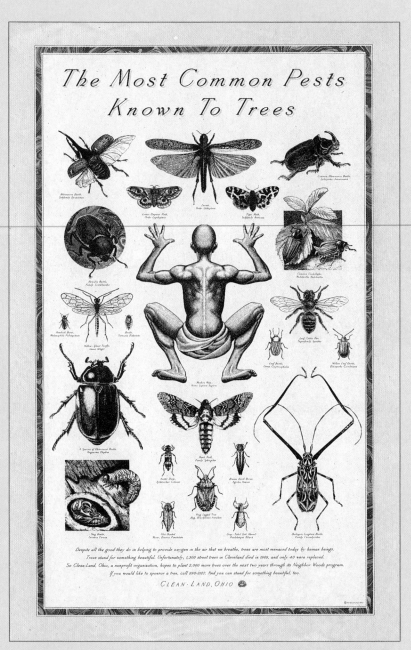

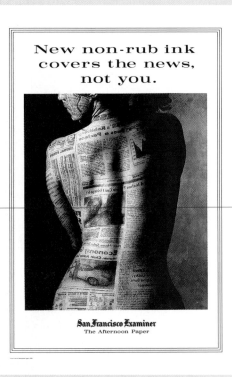

The images in the ads above and at right supply a literal interpretation of the headline in an ingenious, humorous way. The simple black-and-white photos have been given very contrasty lighting (highlights and shadows are intentionally exaggerated) to create beautiful patterns of light and shadow. The result is sophisticated and attention-getting.

The human figure included among and positioned like the insects arouses immediate curiosity. The message is driven home with a creative headline. Copy was kept to a minimum to get the impact from the visual. A delicate typeface and heavy leading for the minimal copy support, not overpower, the visual. This ad could not have worked as well with photographs as it does with the scientific-looking line art. The illustration style adds to the uniqueness of the ad.

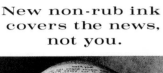

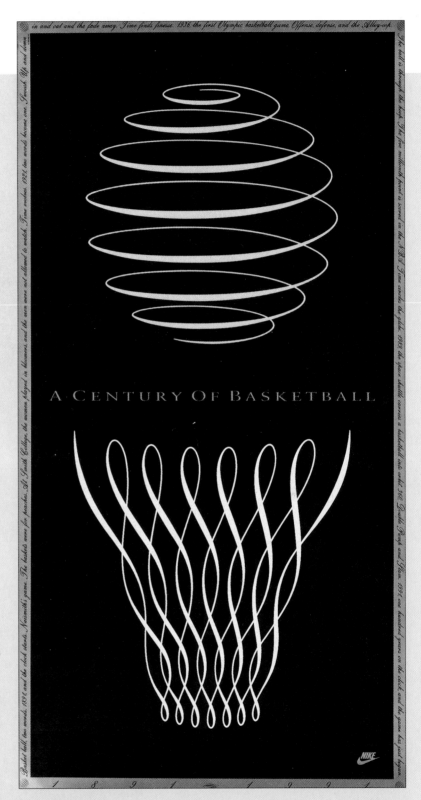

A CENTURY OF BASKETBALL

The designer took a very unique approach to this poster that commemorates "A Century of Basketball." Elegant, calligraphic swooshes that create a basket and ball are quite a departure from the usual photographic treatments used for sports-related pieces. It is memorable, effective and appropriate to the historical nature of the headline. Elegant, yet not feminine, this will still appeal to a predominantly male, sports-minded audience.

Great Headlines+Great Art

You make the greatest impact on readers when you both show and tell them what you want to communicate. That means your layout must be meshed perfectly, both visually and verbally (typographically). Each element should be designed with great care so it is in tune in style and mood with every other element.

A winning combination of type and image should be planned from the start. Choose one main message and make sure both headline and visual drive readers toward it. Give your headline punch with an appropriate type treatment. Then choose a visual that interprets and reinforces your headline. Don't let your headline send one signal and your visual another. Keep your layout as simple and well organized as possible. You'll undermine the impact of a great headline and visual if the piece is so busy the reader doesn't know where to look first. Remember that sometimes a whisper is better than a shout; simplicity, elegance and subtlety play important roles in communication.

A great headline and visual combination isn't always a headline set in large, dramatic type and a gigantic visual. You don't have to make everything big, bold and red to communicate well. A great headline can be set in small type. One or more small pictures can have tremendous impact. You can pair large type with one or more small pictures. You can have a huge picture with a tiny headline. Any layout can produce that memorable, one-two punch of great headline plus great visual—as long as it presents your message in a clear, strong way.

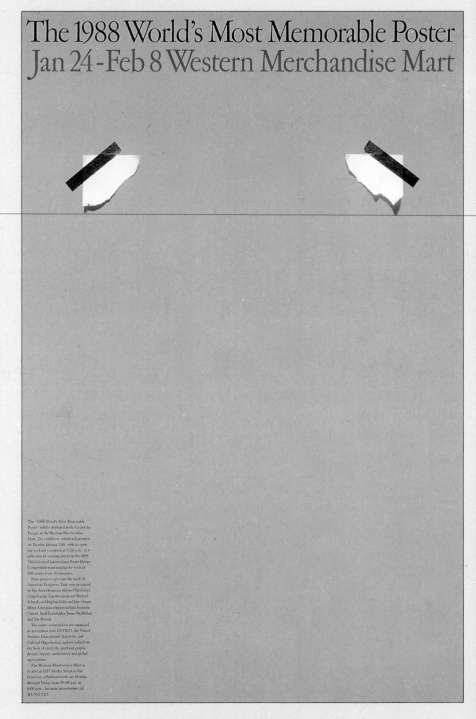

The 1988 World's Most Memorable Poster
Jan 24 - Feb 8 Western Merchandise Mart

The "1988 World's Most Memorable Poster" will be displayed in the Center for Design at the Western Merchandise Mart. The exhibition, which will premiere on Tuesday, January 24th, with an opening cocktail reception at 5:30 p.m., is a collection of winning entries in the 1988 Third Annual International Poster Design Competition representing the work of 800 artists from 40 countries.

Nine posters represent the work of American Designers. Four were produced by Bay Area Designers Michael Vanderbyl, Craig Frazier, Tim Brenton and Michael Schwab, and Stephan Sieler and Jose Ortega. Other American winners include Seymour Chwast, Steff Geissbuhler, James McMullan and Jim Rosock.

The poster competition are organized in association with UNESCO, the United Nations Educational, Scientific and Cultural Organization, and are judged on the basis of creativity, quality of graphic design, impact, authenticity and global appreciation.

The Western Merchandise Mart is located at 1355 Market Street in San Francisco, exhibition hours are Monday through Friday from 10:00 a.m. to 6:00 p.m., for more information call 415/552-2311.

This poster demonstrates that you don't always need elaborate art to make a piece outstanding. You just need a great concept. The simple visual illustrates the headline in an unusual and humorous way for viewers initially attracted by the field of bright yellow.

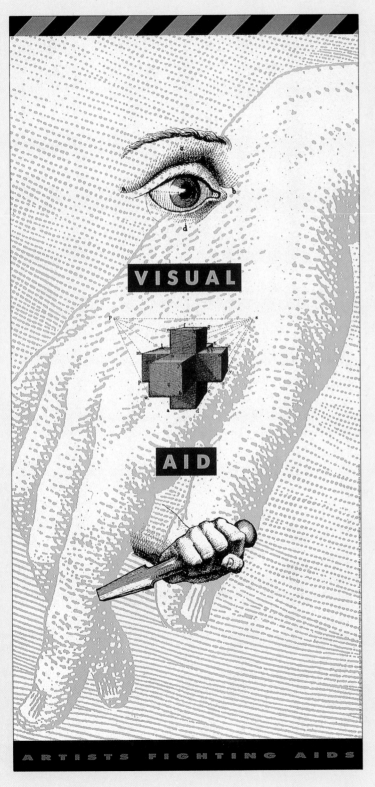

The message of this poster is that artists are uniting to fight AIDS. The slogan "Visual Aid" communicates this message in a new way. The designer used simple woodcut illustrations (probably from a copyright-free source) to depict each word. For example, the eye stands for "visual." A screened back woodcut illustration of a hand behind the main illustrations not only creates a beautiful texture but also adds to the message of giving aid—suggesting giving a helping hand.

Here are some tried-and-true ways to come up with great combinations of headline and art:

• If you can choose the headline, find a very compelling quote or phrase in a book of quotations and work with a stock house specializing in archival photos to find a strong image to communicate that message.

• Find an interesting, engraved style illustration in a book of copyright-free art and enlarge it so the texture of the engraving becomes an abstract pattern. Pair this with one or two words that sum up the message.

• Illustrate a headline about an ordinary object, person or event with a photo showing that subject from an unusual angle or perspective.

• Reinterpret a cliché so it has a new twist. Pair an unexpected visual with a very common phrase.

• If one word in the headline is very important, make it large or use an unusual typeface. Then choose a photo or illustration that depicts that word.

• Overprint type on a photograph so the two work together.

• Outline part of the photo so it extends outside its borders, leading into the type.

• Arrange the type on the opposite page to mimic a shape in the visual.

• Don't forget the power of multiple imagery. A collage of several images can have more impact than a single visual.

• Choose an image that is a visual metaphor for the subject of a piece.

Great Headlines + Great Art

This designer has succeeded in doing the impossible—he has created a beautiful, eye-catching ad with a photo of dipsticks. Even the simplest, most commonplace objects can become visually intriguing when photographed artistically. The play on words in the headline, in which the word "dipstick" is used as a synonym for "idiot," gives the ad extra punch. Never settle for a boring treatment if you must create a layout for a boring subject. Instead, look for ways to give it a distinctive, unexpected twist.

Great headline plus great visual doesn't have to mean one big picture, but can be several smaller ones, as shown here, if they're strong, interesting photos and are given special treatment. The headline is great both verbally and visually. "Flooded" is not only a very visual word but also gives a verbal twist to the message. Notice that the first words of the copy are called out by capitalizing and spreading them across the column width. This ensures that readers will return to the top of the column to start the copy after reading the vertical headline.

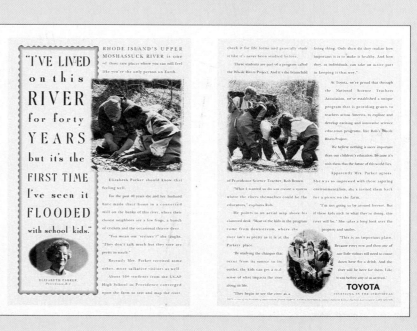

NAME THAT WEED

Crabgrass is just one of many weeds that Pennant® prevents.
So now you can choke out your worst weeds without beating up on
ornamentals and warm-season turf.

P E N N A N T

©1992 CIBA-GEIGY Corporation. Always read and follow label directions.

NAME THAT WEED

Signalgrass is just one of many weeds that Pennant® prevents.
So now you can choke out your worst weeds without beating up on
ornamentals and warm-season turf.

P E N N A N T

©1992 CIBA-GEIGY Corporation. Always read and follow label directions.

NAME THAT WEED

Goosegrass is just one of many weeds that Pennant® prevents.
So now you can choke out your worst weeds without beating up on
ornamentals and warm-season turf.

P E N N A N T

©1992 CIBA-GEIGY Corporation. Always read and follow label directions.

The challenge in the headline—to name common weeds such as crabgrass and goosegrass depicted in unlikely, rather literal interpretations—would quickly arouse the curiosity of most readers. The quirky humor of the ad gives new life to the otherwise dull subject of picking the right herbicide for each weed. When designing your own ads, remember to look at the words and explore new visual translations for them.

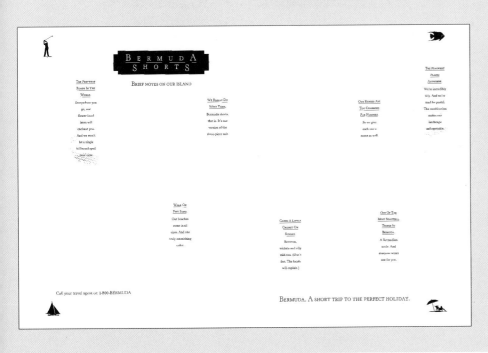

Words often have a double meaning. Taking a simple phrase and then visually communicating the alternate meaning of the words can create a whole new way of looking at something. Because this magazine ad will be read at fairly close range, the illustration of the man wearing Bermuda shorts does not need to be large to make the humor work. The subhead, "Brief Notes on Our Island" and the picture's caption ensure that readers will catch on quickly. Turning the copy into a series of short captions set as short centered lines of type ties in well with the headline.

Great Headlines+Great Art

Men are in crisis, whereas he is not. He does not know the meaning of "crisis." Or perhaps

MR.

BigSHOT

he does, but he pretends otherwise. He is Austrian, after all, and some

By Bill Zehme

Both the headline and the visual are larger than life—just like the article's subject. The powerful image and strong type are perfectly integrated by making the main element in the photo part of the word. This spread is both verbally and visually powerful. The expressive headline demanded a special treatment.

Both the photographic imagery and typography on this spread create a mood of warmth, serenity and classic elegance. The use of classic typefaces and the delicate, small graphic elements reinforce the quiet, elegant feeling. (The elegant look is used here to convey the high quality of a tanker line.) Notice that the designer chose typefaces suggestive of the meaning and the mood of the words in order to create a strong headline. "Smooth" is set in italic, "Sailing" is all caps in a rather nautical looking face, and the whole headline is set off above and below by rules drawn like waves. Also note the contrast between this piece, with its classic look and traditional use of photography, and the nontraditional type and image of the *Rolling Stone* spread on the facing page.

White Space

White space is as necessary to a good layout as copy and visuals. It is the breathing room, the resting places in a layout. White space separates and isolates items so that each can be appreciated in turn. Imagine walking through a museum with paintings crowded on every single inch of wall space. Your eye jumps from piece to piece until you can't tell if the red flowers are planted in a vase or waving on a dog's tail. An overcrowded layout would have the same effect.

White space can be an important design element in its own right. Putting a small headline or visual in the center of a vast expanse of white space emphasizes that small element in an exciting way. Ragging the bottoms of columns gives a layout a more friendly, informal feeling. An unexpected open space adds interest and surprise to a layout.

Sometimes you will have to work hard at finding and arranging white space, especially when laying out a catalog. There are often more products to include than there seems to be space, and each product has copy that "just can't be cut." In these cases, use only enough white space to separate or to group items, and let the rest fall to the edges. Don't leave a big, wasted chunk in the middle. Establish consistent areas of white space from spread to spread, perhaps using a deep top margin to add some air. When cramped for space, reduce the line spacing of your copy to leave more white space around it.

Even though there are many visuals and a lot of descriptive copy on these catalog pages, the designer managed to organize the information in a clear and interesting way. Each caption wraps around its companion image so there can be no doubt what type goes with which picture. The use of very legible, larger red type for product titles draws attention to each copy block. Notice the array of outlined shapes mixed with some square-finished photos. This makes for exciting, lively spreads. Also notice the boxed quote set apart by its heavy, black rule. This copy adds a verbal flavor to the surrounding imagery. Although there isn't a lot of white space because of all the information, the designer placed comfortable amounts of space between the images. Otherwise, everything would be jammed uncomfortably together and readers would be discouraged from browsing through and buying from the catalog.

This catalog has an incredibly clever format. Binding in the center divides the catalog into two categories of products. The inside format is easy to follow with photos opposite the descriptions. Because the designer had minimal copy and photos to include in the piece, generous amounts of white space separate photographs and the short blocks of copy. All the type is loosely leaded. Large margins surround all copy and photo pages. Several photos bleed at least one side and break up the potential "art gallery" look.

Handling white space well is important when working on any project, but it's especially important when you have to produce a piece packed with type and visuals. Here are some tips for making the most of the white space you have—whether it's a little or a lot:

- When cramped for space, use a more condensed face, tighten leading, use smaller margins between columns, and allow space to fall around the edges of the copy.

- Exaggerate the importance of space by surrounding an open area with solid copy. The area of space will stand out.

- On a spread, leave the outer columns open rather than one of the center columns. A space in the center will break continuity.

- Leave a whole ad open with little copy or art to set it off from a copy-heavy newspaper.

- Use equal, open margins across the top of pages to create unity in a brochure.

- Leave a chunk of space crossing two columns of copy and run a callout inside it.

- Use equal amounts of space around type or images to create a balanced, classic look.

- Use unequal amounts of space around visuals to create asymmetry —an energetic feel.

- Leave adequate space for readers to fill out coupons or response cards.

- Contrast a complex image or block of type with a large area of white space.

Copyfitting

Why bother with copyfitting when it's so easy to just pour copy into a computer and get type back? Time and money. You can often salvage the situation if the copy is a little off the targeted length, but there's nothing you can do when it's way off. So, let's see how you go about determining how much copy you have.

First, you need to know the text typeface, the type size in points, how many characters per pica there are (this figure is provided in type reference books), the text column width in picas, the leading in points, and the lines per column inch. The goal is to determine how many typeset words will fit in a vertical column inch of your layout.

Multiply the characters per pica by your column width to learn how many characters fit on one typeset line. Multiply this number by your number of lines per inch to get a total count of characters per column inch. Divide this number by six, the average number of characters in a word, to get the number of words per column inch. Multiply this number times the average number of column inches per page and you'll know how many pages of typeset manuscript you have.

Armed with this information, have the writer produce copy to length whenever possible. If the words come first on a project, use copyfitting to shape an effective layout to fit the copy. For example, you can know right away if you can't use 12-point type because the copy will run twice as many pages as you have.

The client originally gave us this manuscript with each main level of information typed in all caps. The arrangement took up a great deal of space as many labels ran more than one line. Subheads were often run in on the end of a label for a main level of information; the type changed from all caps to upper- and lowercase in the middle of a line.

Remember that any copy provided by your client can be edited (discreetly) and should be restyled in typesetting. If the client wants a word to stand out, you can set it bold or italic for emphasis instead. Define your own styles for heads, subheads, copy, etc. Choose margins, bullets, indents and hyphenation that fit the format of the piece and the overall type design, and use those.

Instruction to printer	Textual mark	Marginal mark
Remove unwanted marks	words and pictures	X
Push down risen spacing material	words and pictures	LOWER
Insert new material	words pictures	∧ and
Delete	words and pictures	ℓ
Delete and close up	words and pictures	ℬ
Correct damaged characters	words and pictures	X
Center type	⌐words and pictures⌐	CENTER
Indent 1 em	⊒ words and pictures	INDENT 1 EM
Delete indent	⌐ words and pictures	FLUSH LEFT
Set type justified	words and pictures ‖	JUSTIFY
Move word up or down	words and pictures	TR
Close up space	words and pictures	⌣
Reduce space between words	words and pictures	REDUCE #
Reduce or insert space between letters	words and pictures	# / ⌒
Close up to normal line spacing	(words and) pictures)	NORMAL #ING
Insert space between paragraphs	words and pictures — The use of type is	#
Reduce space between paragraphs	words and pictures — The use of type is	REDUCE #
Set in or change to italics	words and pictures	ITAL
Set in or change to uppercase	words and pictures	CAP
Set in or change to small capitals	words and pictures	SC
Set in or change to lowercase	words and PICTURES	LC
Set in or change to bold type	words and pictures	BF
Set in or change to bold italic type	words and pictures	BF + ITAL
Insert ligature	encyclopædia	æ
Insert period	words and pictures	⊙
Insert colon	words and pictures	∧ :
Insert semicolon	words and pictures	∧ ;
Insert comma	words and pictures	∧ ,
Insert quotation marks	"words and pictures"	∨ / ∨
Substitute or insert hyphen	words and pictures	∧
New paragraph run in	words and pictures The layout of type is	NO ¶

Paper

The paper your piece is printed on is as essential an element of design as your copy and visuals and should be planned and chosen with the same care. In some pieces the paper is a highly visible aspect of the design, adding color and texture to the overall effect. Paper can also be part of the message. Printing a brochure cover on an elegant cover stock complemented by a high-quality paper inside conveys a sense of richness and success. For other pieces, paper plays more of a supporting role. For example, glossy, high-quality stock helps ensure the excellent reproduction of four-color photographs.

Resist the temptation to keep using the same stock just because it worked on your last piece. It involves more risk and effort to choose something new, but the result can be worth it when you see how a different paper can play a major role in reinforcing the message of your piece. If you want to make a piece stand out, choose an unusual or off-beat paper. Choose an unexpected paper to alter perceptions of a product or service.

Remember that each sheet of paper has its own unique characteristics. Some sheets will perform well when embossed, foil stamped, printed with thermography, varnished or die cut; others won't. So, discuss your plans with your paper merchant and printer, and explore all your options for a project. Just because it's never been done, doesn't mean it can't be.

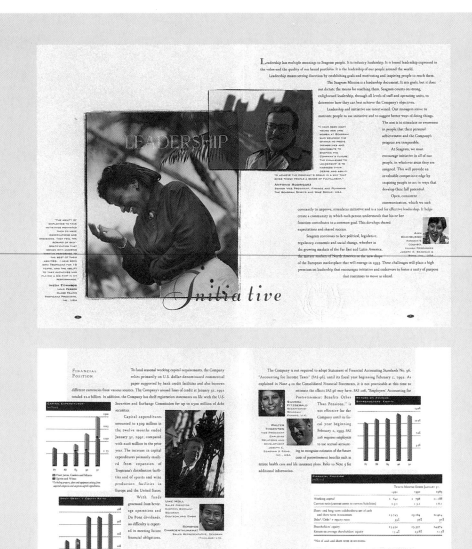

Using recycled paper isn't always an either-or proposition. Many annual reports are printed on recycled paper throughout, but sometimes the right recycled stock for a particular piece just doesn't exist. That doesn't mean you have to give up either your design concept or environmental responsibility. You can print the financial section on recycled paper in one or two colors and print all of the editorial section on a premium paper. This annual report achieves an excellent compromise by using a toothy, uncoated stock for the pages where good four-color reproduction and embossing is needed. A smooth, recycled paper reproduces the various tints and the black-and-white photos in the financial section well.

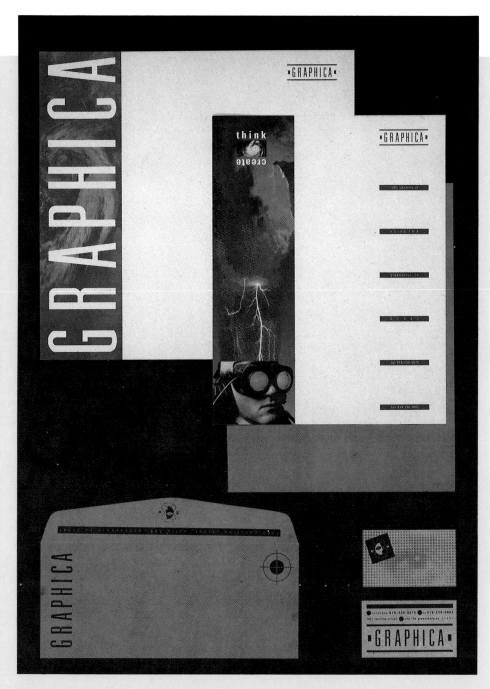

Fibered, recycled paper creates a handcrafted look for this stationery system. The letterhead, business cards, and envelopes each use a different colored, fibered sheet. The system is unified by the use of the same color palette. The back of the letterhead and envelopes are the same color. Although the envelope is printed in only one color, a warm purple, the color of the ink and the dark brown color of the paper combine to create a rich look. The message side of the letterhead is printed on a fairly light-colored sheet in order to get good four-color reproduction for the dramatic visual. The business cards are printed with the same purple as the envelope but are accented with a copper-colored foil stamp that contrasts with the craft paper. Although the card is printed on craft paper, the repro quality of the fairly complex halftone on the back is good due to the use of large dots to make up the image.

Choosing the right paper for a piece can be difficult because there are so many options. Here are some questions you can ask yourself to guide your decision:

• What paper will best help communicate my message?

• What shade and texture do I want?

• What weight do I want? (Remember that using a heavier paper makes a heavier piece that costs more to mail.)

• What character do I want the paper to have? What is appropriate for the audience?

• What paper will best fit the function of this piece? (A brochure that's meant to be read will need a different paper from one meant to create a visual, graphic impression.)

• How much opacity do I need? (Thin, light papers allow the type and visuals printed on one side of the page to show through to the other.)

• What paper will best fit the life span of this piece? (A newsletter that will be kept for reference needs a more durable, higher quality paper than one that will be read and discarded.)

• Is there a recycled stock that's appropriate for this project? (Try to be environmentally responsible whenever possible.)

• What can I afford? Is the paper important enough to this project that I should spend what it takes and look for other savings to offset it?

Mechanicals

The mechanical (the camera-ready, pasted-up assembly of all type and design elements given to the platemaker) is the medium of communication between you and your printer. The mechanical must be clear and accurate: What the camera sees is what you'll get.

Check all measurements carefully before you paste up anything and then position elements precisely. If visuals are incorrectly scaled or improperly placed, they'll be wrong on the plates. If type is broken or improperly aligned, that will show up, too. Cut out the individual lines and blocks of type carefully; sloppy cutting can make the type look crooked, even if it isn't.

Handle all copy, photographs, illustrations and repro with great care. Paste up the mechanical from the top to the bottom so you won't be working over pieces you've already positioned. This reduces the chance that you will move or damage an element. It also lets you see how all the pieces relate to each other.

Be careful when marking and writing instructions to the printer. Clearly mark all color breaks. Write neatly and keep instructions visually separate; your printer should be able to tell which instruction affects what part of the mechanical.

When the mechanical is complete, cover it with heavy paper. Label it with the job name, the date, your name and your phone number and address.

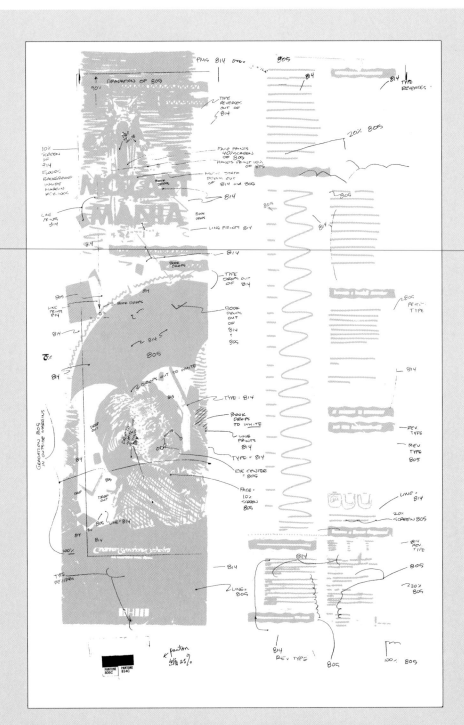

This mechanical had two overlays. One was colored to show precisely where each area of color is. All the written instructions to the printer and the color chips specifying the ink colors to be used appear on a separate overlay. Quantity and paper stock should also be indicated on this overlay.

The board itself has all the type, graphic elements, and "For Position Only" art to show where a separate piece of art is provided. All printer's marks, such as crop marks, are also included on this board. The mechanical was flapped and clearly labeled with the job description, client number and the name, address and phone number of the design firm.

And here is the printed piece.

Here are the steps in preparing a traditional mechanical:

1. Square up the illustration board on your drawing board and secure it. Gather the tools you'll need: a T-square or mayline, a triangle and a photo blue pencil.

2. Indicate with the blue pencil all the grid lines and the placement of type and visuals.

3. Draw all printer's marks in ink. Show crop marks, fold lines, holding lines and bleed lines.

4. Position waxed type on the grid lines and square it up to the base lines.

5. Position and paste down photostats on the mechanical. Make position stats of all color transparencies, photos or other artwork that will be halftoned.

6. After you've pasted up all the elements, make sure your board is clean. It will show up when the board is photographed.

7. If elements overlap each other or run in different colors, position these elements on an acetate overlay.

8. Tape a tissue overlay to the mechanical. Indicate on it what elements print in what color and all notes to the printer.

9. Letter or number each piece of art on a tissue overlay. Label all position stats "For Position Only" (often abbreviated FPO). Attach a tag with the corresponding number or letter to each piece of art with the percentage of enlargement or reduction.

Electronic Mechanicals

When you prepare an electronic mechanical (a page layout file with all necessary printing information), you are responsible for the quality of the output. You must include all the information your service bureau and printer will need in a form that they can use.

Begin any electronic publishing project by consulting with your printer and service bureau. Determine the best form for your mechanical. Sometimes you'll create a file with all type, printer's marks and artwork ready for output directly to film. Other jobs may be part electronic and part traditional mechanical. The right option depends on the project, your desktop skills and the capabilities of your service bureau and printer.

Start with simple electronic mechanicals and work up to more complex jobs involving four-color work and color separations. It takes time and practice to master color corrections and trapping (creating an overlapping area between two colors). (Service bureaus and printers report having to spend more time to fix incorrect traps than they do to create them.)

Prepare your final page layout file carefully. It must be clean and accurate. Include crop and registration marks that print on all pieces of film; having accurate crop marks is critical when doing bleeds. Remove anything that won't be part of the printed piece; even if it doesn't show, it will slow down output at the service bureau. Check all fonts and color specs carefully.

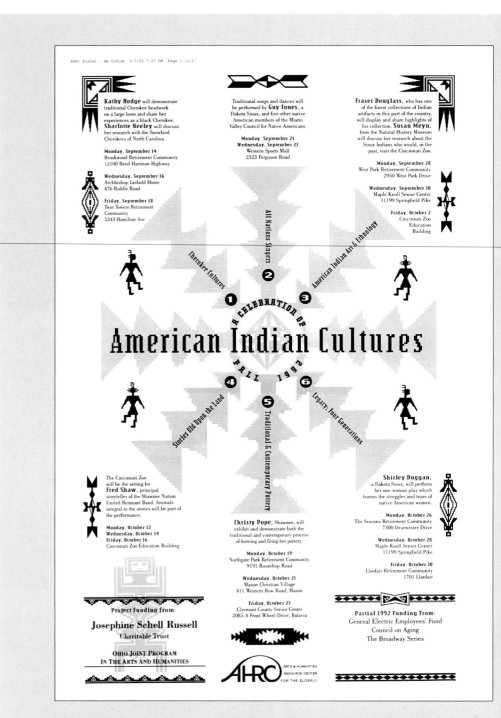

All of the illustrations were created in MacPaint and imported in to QuarkXPress where they were sized and placed. The screens were assigned in Quark after the illustrations were imported, using a 150-line screen. The file was then output to a black-and-white linotronic page on RC paper (commonly called a "lino") with the screens included. The printer made films directly from the linos, using the lino as a halftone positive rather than make and strip in separate halftone negatives. This is a handy technique for low budget projects, because you save the costs of making and stripping any halftone negatives.

Composers for Christmas Concert

AHRC channels professional arts and education programs to the elderly and their historic memories and values back into the community.

The two young composers pictured here have been commissioned by AHRC to write original songs based on what they heard six groups of older people say about their Christmas memories. Participants at *Over-the-Rhine Senior Center*, the *Seasons Retirement Community*, *Merry St.Theresa* and *Arcadia Manor nursing homes*, *Twin Towers Retirement Community* and *Mt. Auburn Senior Center* all gathered in September for large-group sharing sessions on their favorite Christmas memories and what they most value now about Christmas.

The sessions were videotaped and given to the composers so that they can use them as a reference document while they are composing. Five songs by each composer will be performed as AHRC's annual christmas concert.

Alonzo Alexander

THE ARTS & HUMANITIES
RESOURCE CENTER FOR THE ELDERLY

Non-Profit Org.
U.S. Postage
PAID
Cincinnati, Ohio
Permit No. 7274

Arts and Humanities Resource Center
700 Walnut St. Room 310
Cincinnati, Ohio 45202

AUTUMN
1991

Volume 1
Number 1

C·H·A·N·N·E·L·S

The project • CHRISTMAS • *That Silver Time of Year* will be performed:

December 2 .... Seasons Retirement Community
December 4 .... Maple Knoll Village
December 6 .... Union Terminal Auditorium
December 9 .... Twin Towers Retirement Community
December 11 .... Archbishop Leibold Home
December 13 .... Otterbein Home, Lebanon

All concerts will be from 1:30-2:30 p.m. This holiday event will include memories of real lighted candles on Christmas trees - accompanied by buckets of water nearby, oranges in the toe of Christmas stockings, and trudging through snow to midnight Mass and other Christmas services.
Fliers and reservation forms will be available soon.

Before Bill Wahler became AHRC's most popular volunteer, he had a long history of tireless service to older people. A retired circus clown, theater advance-man, and stone mason, Bill offered his services to the Over-the-Rhine Senior Center when it was first getting started in the late sixties.

Ostensibly a transportation volunteer, Bill was on the move from early morning until late at night helping people with grocery shopping, clinic visits, emergency housing, and multiple other social service needs.

When there was a personal crisis, Bill was usually the first person most of the Over-the-Rhine people would call —many times after midnight. Over the years a number of frightened people who called him would hear "Hold on, honey (or old man), I'm coming! I'll meet you at the hospital."

Later, as Director of the Over-the-Rhine Senior Center, he helped to keep the center open on Saturdays and Sundays, creating a warm, friendly place for people to gather. AHRC's first programs occured there in the mid-seventies, and Bill Wahler was an enthusiastic participant and supporter of all aspects of those projects.

Now as he helps at each AHRC program, his compassion and irrepressible good humor welcome people as they get off the buses. The people tell him that when they look out the window and see him standing there, they know they are in a good place. And that's recompense enough for Bill. "After the show is over and I help the people back on the buses, I'm more than happy when they reach out their hand and tell me what a good time they had."

Bill Wahler

Golden Chance Raffle

How does a four-day cruise to Nassau and Freeport sound? Round trip airfare to Miami to board Carnival's luxury ship, the Fantasy, is all included in the first prize of AHRC's Golden Chance Raffle. The ten other prizes are all exciting: $700 set of luggage, a weekend at the Clarion Hotel, a microwave oven, dinner for two at the Maisonette, a gold necklace, a Rookwood vase, a case of selected wines, dinner for two at the Palace Restaurant, two Broadway Series tickets, and two Playhouse in the Park tickets.

This raffle will replace a much more expensive fund-raising event. The limited printing of 1500 tickets makes the $10 ticket price enticing since most of the prizes are for two.

Call the AHRC office for tickets (579-1074). The drawing will be held December 6.

Did you know that in the past year AHRC provided 138 programs for an audience of 10,823 elderly from 81 facilities?

The document was created in QuarkXPress. All of the type, rules and dots were created in the program as part of the page layout file. The photos were scanned as halftones, saved as TIFF files and imported into Quark where they were sized and positioned. The large piano illustration was scanned as line art, saved as a TIFF file and imported into Quark where it was sized and screened back to 20 percent. In order to make the type print over the piano illustration, the background of the text box was set to "None." The picture box holding the illustration was assigned "No Runaround" and "Send to Back." Choosing "No Runaround" kept the type from wrapping around the illustration while "Send to Back" prevented the type from disappearing behind the illustration.

Here are the steps in preparing an electronic mechanical:

1. Create the final page layout.

2. Specify any spot or custom colors to be used. Use a color matching system for spot color; screen colors are often inaccurate.

3. Scan any photos and illustrations and incorporate them into the page layout file. Placement of artwork may be indicated by holding lines.

4. Integrate final type and design elements.

5. Proof the piece. Make any needed corrections and output proofs to send to the service bureau.

6. Check the layout for and remove any unwanted fonts and guidelines. Remove everything from the clipboard.

7. Review the job with the service bureau and printer.

8. Send all necessary files to the service bureau with the actual layout file. Supply all images to be used including all scans, illustrations and color separations (unless these are being handled conventionally). Include any special fonts the service bureau will need.

9. Send along the proof and a job sheet. The job sheet should have your name, phone number, the job name and the date by which you need it. Identify the submission format, the name and version number of your page layout program, then names and manufacturers of all fonts used, and the names and graphic formats (TIFF, PICT, EPS) of all graphics.

A Few Last Words

In this chapter we've looked at the many options for combining the building blocks, type and visuals, into good layouts. And we've looked at some of the basics of getting your piece ready to be printed—cropping and scaling, fixing poor quality photos, copyfitting, selecting paper, and preparing both traditional and electronic mechanicals.

The most important thing to remember about making a good layout is to communicate clearly. Before the finished piece can communicate its message to the intended audience, you must have communicated clearly with everyone else working on the project (co-worker, copywriter, photographer, illustrator), the client (creating pieces for yourself is no more straightforward than producing work for others) and the printer and color separator or service bureau—those who must execute your design in print.

Think through everything you want to do and plan how to do it. Consult your printer, service bureau operator, or paper merchant or a paper mill rep if you're not sure how to achieve an effect you want. Many times they will be able to help you get what you want at a price you can afford.

Never be afraid to explore using a new paper or technique. Designers and printers used to think that quality printing on kraft paper was impossible; it's common practice now. But do find out how it can be done and what it will cost before you invest a great deal of time incorporating that paper or technique into your project. It's harder to let go of a wonderful idea that isn't practical for time or budgetary reasons after you've done a lot of work on it than it is when you're working out preliminary sketches.

Asking questions can save you and your client money. The size of a piece and how it fits on the press can dramatically affect cost. Pieces that are multiples of 8½"x11" (4¼"x5½", 11"x17", etc.) fit paper sizes and presses most effectively.

Paper merchants will provide printed samples and folded dummies demonstrating how papers will look and feel—and how they will print. Check your paper choice with your printer. Adjustments may have to be made to the separations if the paper you want is colored or uncoated and highly absorbent. If you start with a bad quality photo and print it on an uncoated, colored stock, you will end up with mud.

If the piece will be mailed, check into postal regulations. Otherwise you may spend a lot of money producing something that is very costly or impossible to mail. The postal service can sometimes help you save money—having your mailing sorted by zip code or bar coded to postal specifications can reduce mailing costs.

Chapter 4
More Good Examples

There are as many good ways to work with words and pictures as there are good designers. This chapter presents different types of pieces done by a variety of designers to introduce numerous options for making good layouts. You'll get ideas for ways you can make what you've learned in this book work on any kind of project. You'll also see experimental, unique approaches that serve as a springboard to extend the design boundaries of your own layouts.

The work of outstanding designers like these whose work is displayed here is a great source of inspiration. You may find a type treatment you've never considered using before. You may discover an intriguing visual interpretation of a headline. Start building on these ideas and approaches, and your visual vocabulary and repertoire of layout techniques will expand. It's a great way to grow, constantly improving the way you work with words and pictures. Remember, take in everything around you and experiment, experiment, experiment!

This chapter showcases outstanding newsletters, posters, brochures, letterheads, ads, logos and packaging that demonstrate a range of options to explore in your own designs.

Logos

A unique logotype can grow from one small change in a letterform. Changing from uppercase to lowercase *e*'s and then tilting them so they look like eyes produces a typographic visual that playfully communicates the meaning of the word.

CHINESE LAUNDRY

[WORLDWIDE
OPERATIONS]

[MISSION
STATEMENT]

[STRATEGIC
INITIATIVES]

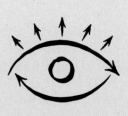

[VALUES]

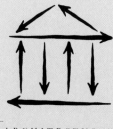

[ARCHITECTURAL
DIRECTION]

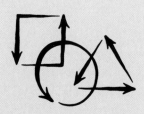

[COMPONENTS]

An arrow hand-drawn in a sketchy technique is the basis for this unique, unified system of symbols. Each symbol is primarily composed of arrows and has its title centered within brackets. At the same time, each symbol distinctively represents the concept implied in the title. The designer has come up with a simple, lively system that makes an original use of a basic graphic element.

I DREAM A WORLD

The designer played with the size, style and placement of the lettering to create a logotype where visual and meaning are perfectly married. The designer has transformed the initials of the client, who is a watchmaker, into a simple, elegant watch's face. Type has become art in a memorable, unique image that clearly communicates its message.

The illustration style of this logo for the eleventh annual conference of the National Court Appointed Special Advocate Association is very appropriate. It is primitive and childlike, almost like a children's book illustration, an excellent choice for an organization committed to fighting for the dream of safe and permanent homes for abused and neglected children. The star, a traditional symbol of hope, becomes the focal point because all the children are pointing to it.

The letterforms of this logo are invertible—turn it either way up and it still reads the same. To achieve this, the designer developed distinctive abstractions of the letterforms. The word has become more than a word; it is now a memorable graphic for this company.

Ads

If You Don't Help A Boy Discover Wildlife, Somebody Else Will.

It's a jungle out there for kids. Drugs. Alcohol. Sex. Crime. They need help to survive in the wild—or they may never be out of the woods. Scouting puts boys on the right path. Gives them the sense of belonging they need. Offers them adventure. And positive role models. But it takes volunteers like you. You don't need experience. We'll show you the ropes. All you need is a desire to make a difference in the life of a boy. It's fun—and rewarding. Find out how you can help. Call the Boy Scouts at 251-5322. And help a boy to be prepared when he hears the call of the wild.

Boy Scouts of America

(Left) The headline of this ad features a clever play on words, capitalizing on the two very different meanings of the word *wildlife.* These two meanings are then clearly illustrated by the large visual to ensure readers get the message. Readers drawn in by the intriguing verbal/visual word play will then be motivated to read the rest of the message and respond to the call to action. The Boy Scout logo, which is actually a photograph of their badge, is set off with tons of white space at the bottom to make sure readers notice it. Note the repetition of the Boy Scout symbol throughout the ad—on the shirt, the knife, a patch and the slide.

You don't need four-color visuals to create a memorable ad. Here the visual gives a twist to the simple words in the headline to make the reader of this newspaper ad do a double take. The ad's copy, below the visual, then clarifies the message using the minimum copy necessary to make its pitch. The rolls of paper are shown standing on end, which isn't how you usually see them, to take advantage of the vertical space and to pull the reader down to the copy at the bottom.

Free breakfast rolls.

Buy two months of the Birmingham Post-Herald, get one month free.
Call 323-6397.

Suggested rates for participating distributors of carrier delivery areas. Mail rates quoted upon request. Offer good only with pre-paid subscriptions through the Circulation Department. For new subscribers only.

The best advertising attracts people naturally. Because it evolves from a very natural process. First, knowing who your customer is and how your product is related. Then crafting a strategy that skillfully links the two. And finally, presenting the right message in a manner so compelling, the right people are drawn to it willingly. Most advertising agencies know this process. But none follow it more instinctively than Northlich Stolley LaWarre.

Northlich Stolley LaWarre
Advertising, Public Relations, 200 West Fourth Street, Cincinnati, Ohio 45202 (513) 421-8840

The typography becomes part of the visual, leading the eye to the central image. The type treatment turns the copy into the shape of the trail of the moth, thereby demonstrating the agency's creativity. The large amount of white space separates the ad from other items in the crowded newspaper environment and showcases the visual.

Newsletters

The use of screened-back background textures provides a nice contrast to the very clean format of this newsletter. The four-column grid permits a lot of flexibility in the sizing and placement of visuals. Sometimes a column is left partially open to add white space and give the piece an airy feel. The columns hang on the same grid line at the top, but they rag at the bottom creating a nice, casual rhythm.

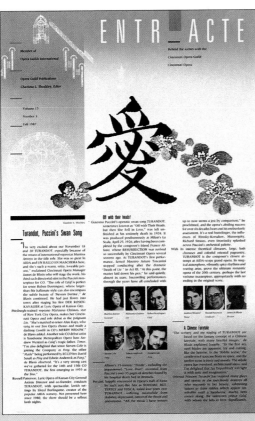
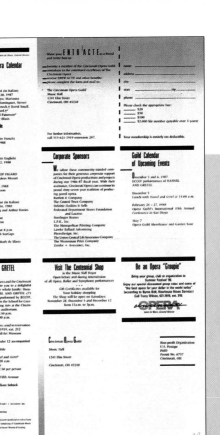

This newsletter has a beautiful consistent typographic system. The designer uses rules, unusual indents and soft gradations consistently throughout the piece to give every element on the page a distinctive look. The white space created between columns interrupted by hanging the first line of each paragraph into it effectively leads the reader through the copy.

Brochures

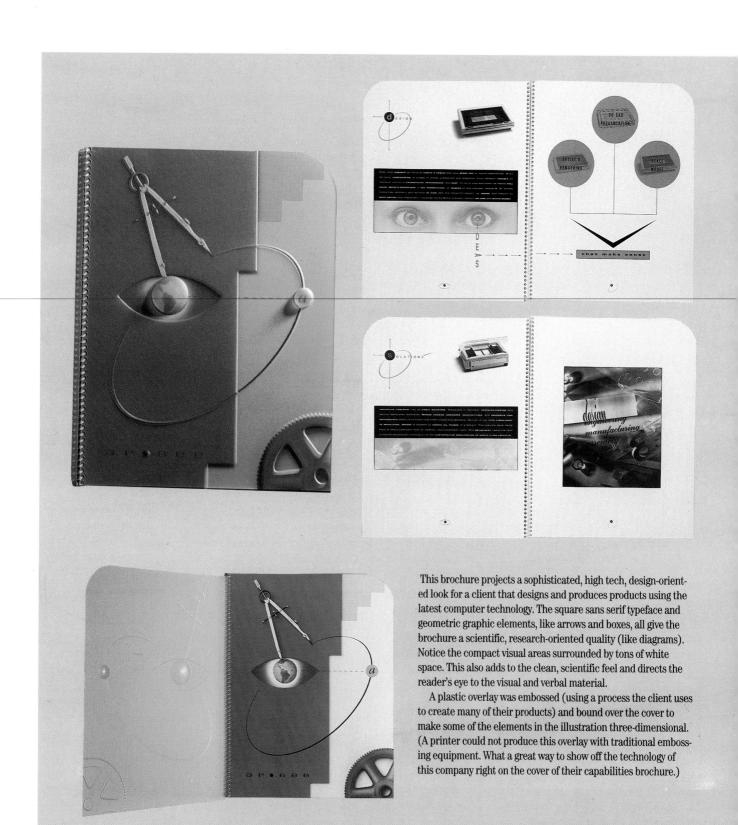

This brochure projects a sophisticated, high tech, design-oriented look for a client that designs and produces products using the latest computer technology. The square sans serif typeface and geometric graphic elements, like arrows and boxes, all give the brochure a scientific, research-oriented quality (like diagrams). Notice the compact visual areas surrounded by tons of white space. This also adds to the clean, scientific feel and directs the reader's eye to the visual and verbal material.

A plastic overlay was embossed (using a process the client uses to create many of their products) and bound over the cover to make some of the elements in the illustration three-dimensional. (A printer could not produce this overlay with traditional embossing equipment. What a great way to show off the technology of this company right on the cover of their capabilities brochure.)

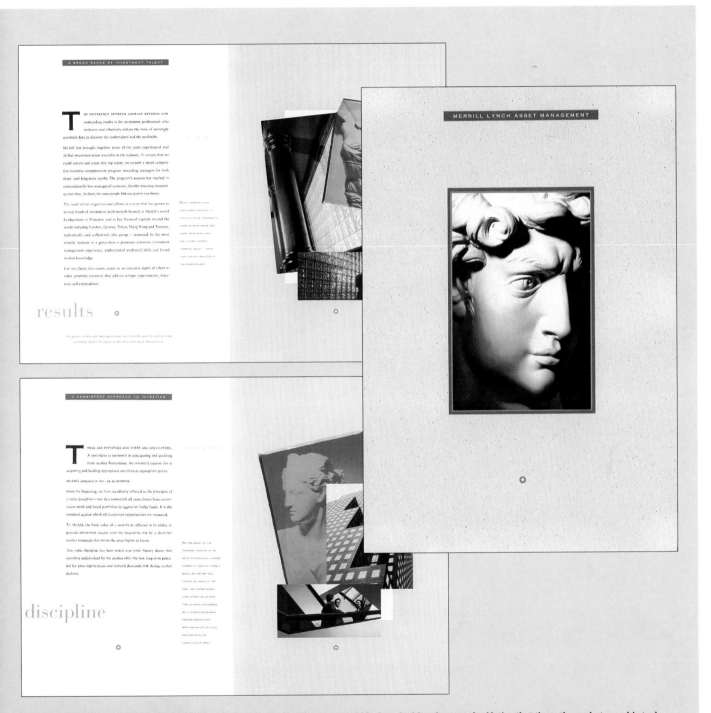

The collage imagery on these spreads combines Polaroid transfers, duotones and black-and-white photographs. Notice that these three photographic techniques are used in the images on every spread for consistency but the arrangements change to add variety. The use of the sculptural images gives the piece a classical feel. Combining classical sculpture with more modern images communicates the message that Merrill Lynch Asset Management builds on past success to help create a strong future. Key words are called out and float in the white spaces on the page. These give the readers a quick message and promote further investigation of the copy. Excerpts from a speech are separated from the body copy by type style, size and color. The reader is given small, bite-sized chunks of copy surrounded by plenty of open, white space to show the reader this material can be quickly and easily read.

Brochures

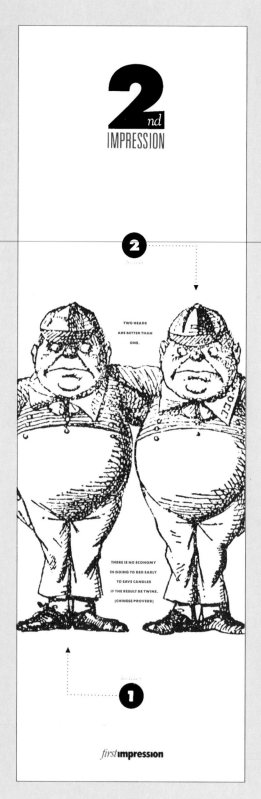

2nd
IMPRESSION

TWO HEADS
ARE BETTER THAN
ONE.

THERE IS NO ECONOMY
IN GOING TO BED EARLY
TO SAVE CANDLES
IF THE RESULT BE TWINS.
[CHINESE PROVERB]

*first*impression

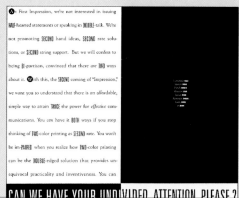

At First Impression, we're not interested in issuing HALF-hearted statements or speaking in DOUBLE-talk. We're not promoting SECOND hand ideas, SECOND rate solutions, or SECOND string support. But we will confess to being BI-partisan, convinced that there *are* TWO ways about it. With this, the SECOND coming of "Impression," we want you to understand that there is an affordable, simple way to attain TWICE the power for *effective* communications. You can have it BOTH ways if you stop thinking of TWO-color printing as SECOND rate. You won't be im-PAIRED when you realize how TWO-color printing can be the DOUBLE-edged solution that provides un-equivocal practicality and inventiveness. You can

CAN WE HAVE YOUR UNDIVIDED ATTENTION PLEASE?

achieve infinite *creativity* and produce *economical* communications with a mere TWO colors. There is nothing BI-partisan about our BI-ased point of view. BI-form printing need not BI-furcate the effect you want to achieve *(figure that one out!)*. You'll be dancing the TWO-step when you re-DEUCE your constraints, re-DOUBLE your efforts and COUPLE your imagination with TWO-color printing that is SECOND to none. How did we come to this TWO-dimensional view? By understanding the power of TWOS in all areas of our lives. TWOS are synonymous with unheralded accomplishments throughout human history. Therefore, we dedi... the power of TWOS, particular...

The comical illustration of Twee-dle-Dee and Tweedle-Dum on the cover is a fun play on the title of the publication and sets the tone for the whole piece. The fun, humorous mood of the piece is carried through in the varied typefaces used on a spread—and in one place, run on angle, odd looking copyright-free illustrations and flu-orescent colors. The copy is a lively mixture of humorous stories, com-mentary and poetry related to the theme of "twoness." Each spread becomes a unique interpretation of the copy in image and type. The piece is full of surprises, holding the reader's attention throughout.

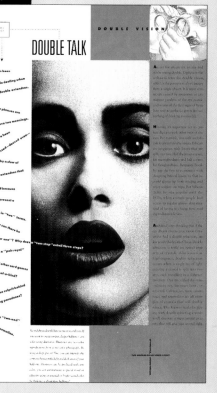

f a m i l y

Family photos are the focal points of this tribute to families. The combination of the soft duotones and the poetic copy set in attractive typographic arrangements creates a beautiful, engaging brochure. This self-promotion piece was meant to be a gift that recipients would treasure. The small size, the special binding and the emotional subject matter give the readers something they can't help becoming involved with. Notice that the typographic treatment changes from spread to spread as it interprets the copy. Setting the type in a circle and calling out special words in size and color makes a nice marriage of type and message.

family become friends. There are no straight paths. only circles of understanding where friends become family. family become friends.

Wishing my child
to know the family
i came to know.

Holding fingers.

walking boldly with "boppa".

Gentle "nanny"

tugging at my imagination

with fairy tales and fables.

Teasing cousins. sassy aunts and winking uncles

challenging

me with twice-told tales of family adventures.

DO I UNDERSTAND THE LIFE-LONG WISDOM

THAT ANSWERED MY CHILD-LIKE WONDER?

Letterheads

The logo is blown up very large to form an interesting screened-back background on the stationery. The logo has a very strong architectural, geometric quality that becomes a strong statement when enlarged. It's an appropriate look for this client who is an expert at assembling various office panel systems, a task that requires precision and craftsmanship. Notice that the address is set justified in keeping with this very geometric feel. The envelope does not use the screened-back background and has been carefully laid out to comply with postal regulations.

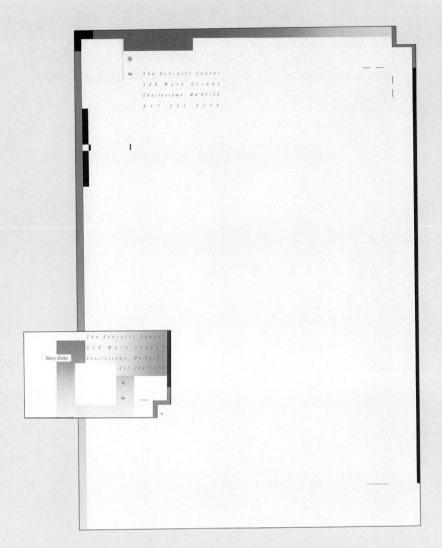

Gradations, dashed lines, blocks of color, die cut corners and a small yellow circle become the graphic language of this stationery system. (A graphic language is a series of consistent graphic elements used to hold a layout together.) Notice that the letterhead sheet, the business card and the envelope use the same elements but the layout and placement change from piece to piece. Therefore it is both consistent and varied. Some of the dashes are functional, indicating margins to the typist.

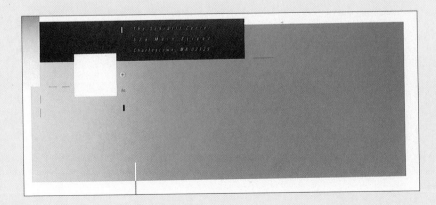

Letterheads

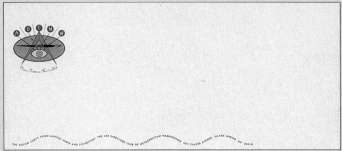

This whimsical letterhead system showcases a playful texture, type and a variety of visuals. The *A* formed by futuristic shapes becomes the focal point from which the rest of the composition radiates. The address information is set in rippled type that echoes the border. Although the border isn't repeated on the envelope, the line of ripple type helps tie the pieces together.

This letterhead demonstrates that you don't need more than one color to create an effective, unique letterhead. The logo is a great use of shape to convey a stylized face that is using its hand to stifle a giggle—a perfect visual for the company's name. The stylized products create a wrapping paperlike texture over the back of the letterhead.

Posters

This is a perfect party poster in which many elements combine to suggest a feeling of fun and excitement. The illustration in the center is childlike and suggestive of fun. The designer played with scale by blowing up the central characters and varnishing them over a black background. Notice that there is no specific orientation to the poster. You can rotate and hang it anyway you like. The small descriptive phrases entice readers to explore them because they create interesting curves and angles and are surrounded by vast amounts of black. The type appears to dance around the page.

Borders, texture and an illustration style reminiscent of Picasso's work make this poster visually intriguing. The square, rigid border provides a nice contrast to the loose, flowing illustration, but notice that the illustration does occasionally break the border to add excitement. Because the poster as a whole is dark, the areas of red and yellow-orange pop and catch the eye.

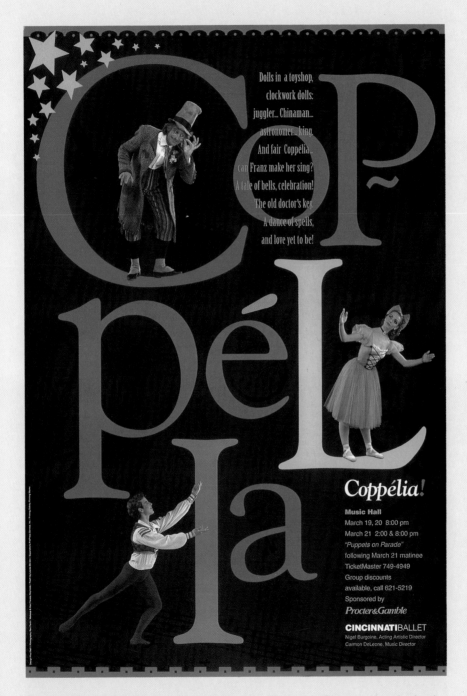

The title of the ballet itself becomes the main element in the visual on this poster. Note also that the title has been carefully broken into syllables and an accent placed over the *e* to help those unfamiliar with the title pronounce it. The designer had fun dropping silhouetted photos of the main characters into the empty spaces within the letterforms. The title treatment and the inset visuals tell something about the personality of the ballet rather than just its title.

Posters

The image of the woman screaming grabs the viewer's attention and communicates the title of the design lecture series, "The Radical Response." The jagged, red shape attracts the eye to the emotional expression of the person in the photograph as well as symbolizing the scream. The textures of the image and the background for the type add even more excitement and activity. The hand-drawn lettering is perfect for the impromptu quality of the poster.

Leaving the poster mostly white symbolizes winter—very appropriate for a poster announcing winter class registration. The crisp, black type has been set justified in a block that creates a nice contrast of shape with the organic, outlined shape of the skater. The designer has used lines and little, triangular shapes around the skater to suggest motion. Also notice how the type gets progressively smaller as you read the paragraph. The larger beginning lines grab you and lead you into the rest of the message.

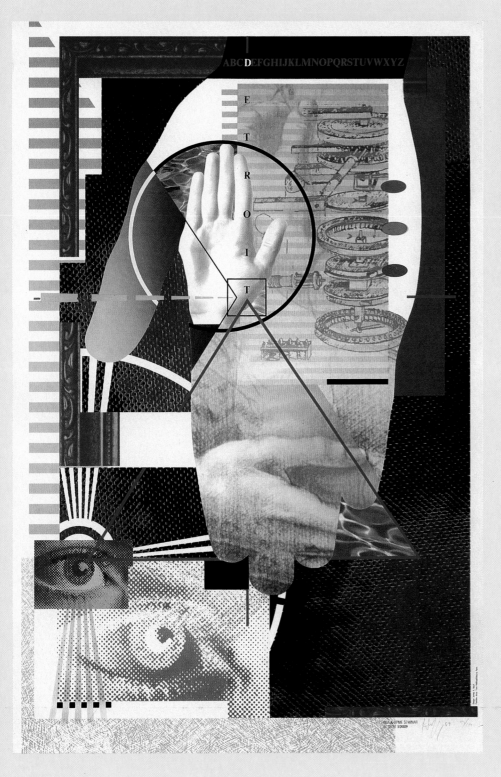

This poster for a Detroit BDA & BPME seminar projects a very futuristic, computerized look. The designer unified the very complex image by selecting several elements to be repeated throughout the poster. The shape of the hand, the shape of the eye, the repeated thick bands and dot patterns serve as this visual glue. A very strong focal point is created in the center, where the word "Detroit" converges with several large graphic elements. This highly visual message has very little copy, and that copy has a subtle treatment. The designer could be more innovative and less direct with the message because he was communicating with fellow design professionals.

Packaging

The designer took a new approach to showing the product on the packaging. A Converse shoe was shot from each of the angles it would be seen from if the box were transparent. Then each silhouetted halftone (the halftone dots around the image have been removed so the image appears on a white background) was tilted to create a loose, fun feeling. The space around the image is activated by the tilt. Angled areas of white are created rather than static, straight shapes.

A posterized (high contrast) image of a baseball player becomes the background for this soap packaging. An athlete needs an extra strength soap, so tying that image to the product really works. The natural paper label reminiscent of nineteenth century health product ads creates an intriguing contrast with the background. Rules, borders and boxes are used to separate areas of information and to separate copy from illustration on the label. They are also very appropriate for the period feel the designer was trying to create.

The designer combined photos from old movies with an art deco graphic treatment when designing this series of labels. This approach both suggests sophistication and evokes nostalgia from the product's audience. Although a range of shapes and colors are used, the labels are tied together by their common theme, the linking of the product's name with a large, triangular shape, and the circular "collector's series" symbol that appears on each.

The elegant, naturalistic drawings reminiscent of botanical illustrations link all the different product packages in this line. The typography—very clean, classic and elegant—complements the illustrations. All the packaging is made from environmentally sound materials, an important consideration when the client is an organization dedicated to preserving tropical and rain forests.

More Good Examples

Index